THE MIND-BODY Connection

How Your Physical Health Shapes Your Mindset

M L Rusenak

Copyright © 2023 by Trient Press

All rights reserved. No part of this publication may be reproduced, distributed, or transmitted in any form or by any means, including photocopying, recording, or other electronic or mechanical methods, without the prior written permission of the publisher, except in the case of brief quotations embodied in critical reviews and certain other noncommercial uses permitted by copyright law. For permission requests, write to the publisher, addressed "Attention: Permissions Coordinator," at the address below.

Criminal copyright infringement, including infringement without monetary gain, is investigated by the FBI and is punishable by up to five years in federal prison and a fine of $250,000.

Except for the original story material written by the author, all songs, song titles, and lyrics mentioned in the novel The Mind-Body Connection: How Your Physical Health Shapes Your Mindset are the exclusive property of the respective artists, songwriters, and copyright holder.

Trient Press
3375 S Rainbow Blvd
#81710, SMB 13135
Las Vegas, NV 89180

Ordering Information:
Quantity sales. Special discounts are available on quantity purchases by corporations, associations, and others. For details, contact the publisher at the address above.
Orders by U.S. trade bookstores and wholesalers. Please contact Trient Press: Tel: (775) 996-3844; or visit www.trientpress.com.

Printed in the United States of America

Publisher's Cataloging-in-Publication data
Ruscsak, M.L.
A title of a book :The Mind-Body Connection: How Your Physical Health Shapes Your Mindset
ISBN
Hardcover   979-8-88990-075-7
Paperback   979-8-88990-076-4
E-book   979-8-88990-077-1

"THE MIND-BODY CONNECTION: HOW YOUR PHYSICAL HEALTH SHAPES YOUR MINDSET": GUIDE AND WORKBOOK

Introduction:

Chapter 1: The Link Between Physical Health and Mental Health
Chapter 2: Exercise and Mental Health
Chapter 3 mental health after a life-changing event
Chapter 4: Nutrition and Mental Health
Chapter 5: Sleep and Mental Health
Chapter 6: Lifestyle Changes for a Positive Mindset

The mind-body connection is a concept that has been explored by scientists and philosophers for centuries. This chapter will define the mind-body connection and explain how physical health affects mindset.

What is the Mind-Body Connection?

The mind-body connection refers to the relationship between a person's thoughts, emotions, and behaviors and their physical health. It suggests that the mind and body are not separate entities but are interconnected and interdependent.

According to this theory, a person's thoughts and emotions can affect their physical health and vice versa. For example, stress and anxiety can cause physical symptoms such as headaches and muscle tension, while chronic physical pain can lead to depression and anxiety.

How Physical Health Affects Mindset

Physical health is closely linked to mental health and can have a significant impact on a person's mindset. Here are a few examples:

Exercise and Mood

Exercise has been shown to have a positive impact on mood and can help reduce symptoms of depression and anxiety. This is because exercise releases endorphins, which are natural chemicals that boost mood and reduce pain.

Nutrition and Cognitive Function

A healthy diet that includes fruits, vegetables, whole grains, and lean protein can provide the nutrients needed for optimal brain function. On the other hand, a poor diet that is high in sugar and processed foods can lead to cognitive impairment, including memory problems and difficulty concentrating.

Sleep and Mental Health

Getting enough sleep is essential for good mental health. Chronic sleep deprivation can lead to mood swings, irritability, and difficulty concentrating. It can also increase the risk of developing depression and anxiety.

In conclusion, the mind-body connection is a complex concept that suggests that physical health and mental health are intertwined. Physical health can affect mood, cognitive function, and overall mental well-being. By understanding the mind-body connection, individuals can take steps to improve their physical health and, in turn, improve their mindset.

My personal story about how physical health impacted mindset

Physical health is an essential aspect of overall well-being, and it can have a significant impact on a person's mindset. I have experienced this firsthand in my own life. In this chapter, I will share my story of how physical health impacted my mindset.

My Story

In this chapter, I'd like to share my personal story about how physical health impacted my mindset. For years, I never realized that my mindset could affect my health, and it took a long time for me to understand this connection.

Let's start in 2010-2011, when I was 28 years old, married with a wonderful daughter, and working a job that I mostly enjoyed. On the outside, I was the PTO mom who volunteered at my daughter's school and always had a smile on my face. But deep down, I was struggling with depression as my marriage was failing, and my daughter's autism made her younger years particularly stressful for me.

The stress continued to build up, and before long, my health started to decline rapidly. Now there were some outside reasons that accelerated the decline but that is discussed in the "Hope, healing and Rising Strong" series. For today I would like to focus on my mindset.

While my health was declining, I experienced two strokes, and my depression even led to cluster seizures, respiratory issues, and cardiac problems. Even as some of the more noticeable symptoms got better, other health issues began to surface.

After my second failed marriage, I realized that I needed to focus on healing myself before anything else. I started by adding a daily exercise program to my routine, changing my diet, and taking steps to find happiness in my life. And as I did, I began to see real improvements in my health.

One of the first changes I made was to incorporate exercise into my daily routine. At first, it was difficult, and I struggled to find the motivation to get up and move my body. However, I found that once I got started, it became easier and easier, and I actually began to enjoy it. The exercise helped me to release pent-up stress and anxiety, and I found that it also helped to clear my mind and improve my focus. I started to feel better physically, and I also noticed a shift in my mindset. I began to feel more positive and optimistic about the future, and I started to believe that things could get better.

In addition to exercise, I also made changes to my diet. I cut out processed foods and started eating more fruits, vegetables, and lean protein. I also started paying more attention to the quality and quantity of my sleep. I made sure to get at least 7-8 hours of sleep each night, and I started practicing relaxation techniques like meditation and deep breathing. As I made these changes, I noticed that my physical health continued to improve, and my mental health also started to improve. I felt more energized and focused, and I also felt more in control of my emotions.

Over time, I began to realize that my physical health and mental health were interconnected. When I took care of my body, my mind also benefited, and vice versa. As I continued to make these changes, I started to feel like a different person. I was more confident, more resilient, and more positive. I started to believe that I could overcome the challenges in my life, and I started to see the world in a more positive light.

In conclusion, my personal story is just one example of how physical health can impact mindset. When we take care of our bodies, we also take care of our minds. Exercise, diet, and sleep are all important factors that can contribute to improved mental health. It is important to recognize that physical and mental health are interconnected, and that taking care of both is essential for overall well-being.

Journal Exercises

Reflect on a time when you felt like your physical health was negatively impacting your mindset. What were the specific symptoms you experienced?

_____
_____
_____
_____
_____
_____
_____
_____

How did it affect your day-to-day life? Write about any changes you made to improve your physical health and how it affected your mindset.

Think about your current physical health habits. Are you getting enough sleep, exercise, and proper nutrition? Write about any areas where you feel like you could make improvements and make a plan to implement changes.

_____
_____
_____
_____
_____
_____
_____
_____
_____
_____
_____
_____
_____
_____
_____
_____

Write down 3-5 things that make you feel stressed or overwhelmed. Then, brainstorm ways you could alleviate these stressors through physical health habits. For example, if you feel stressed about work, you could plan to take a walk during your lunch break to get some fresh air and exercise.

_____
_____

Make a list of physical health goals that align with improving your mindset. These could include things like getting more sleep, eating more whole foods, or trying a new form of exercise. Write about how achieving these goals could positively impact your mindset.

Reflect on the times when you have felt most energized, focused, and motivated. What were you doing during those times?

Did your physical health habits play a role in how you felt? Write about how you can replicate those feelings by making conscious choices to prioritize your physical health.

Personal Survey

On a scale of 1 to 5, how often do you experience stress or anxiety? How often do you exercise per week?

Do you believe that your physical health affects your mental health?

How many hours of sleep do you typically get per night?

On a scale of 1 to 5, how satisfied are you with your current level of physical health?

Have you ever made changes to your physical health in an effort to improve your mental health? If yes, what changes did you make and did you notice any improvements in your mental health?

How important do you think self-care is in maintaining a positive mindset?

Have you ever tried any mindfulness or relaxation techniques (e.g., meditation, yoga) to improve your mental health? If yes, what techniques have you tried and did you find them helpful?

What other factors do you think contribute to a positive mindset?

Are you interested in learning more about the mind-body connection and how you can improve your mental health through physical health practices?

What is the mind-body connection?
a) The belief that the mind and body are separate and have no influence on each other.
b) The belief that physical health has no effect on mental health.
c) The idea that the mind and body are connected and have a significant impact on each other's health.

How can physical activity benefit your mental health?
a) By increasing stress levels and inducing anxiety.
b) By reducing the production of endorphins, the "feel-good" chemicals in the brain.
c) By increasing the production of endorphins, reducing stress, and boosting mood.

What effect does poor sleep have on mental health?
a) It has no effect.
b) It can increase the risk of depression, anxiety, and other mental health problems.
c) It can improve mental clarity and focus.

Can diet impact mental health?
a) No, diet has no impact on mental health.
b) Yes, diet can influence mood, energy levels, and overall mental health.
c) Diet only affects physical health, not mental health.

How can practicing mindfulness benefit mental health?
a) By increasing anxiety and stress levels.
b) By decreasing focus and productivity.

c) By reducing stress, increasing focus, and improving overall mental well-being.

CHAPTER 1: THE LINK BETWEEN PHYSICAL HEALTH AND MENTAL HEALTH

Physical health and mental health have long been recognized as interconnected, with the mind-body connection being the subject of much research in recent years. While it has been known for centuries that physical and mental health are linked, the scientific understanding of this relationship has only become clearer in recent decades. This chapter will explore the connection between physical health and mental health, discussing the evidence supporting this relationship and its implications for individuals and society as a whole.

The Physical Health-Mental Health Connection

The mind-body connection is based on the idea that mental and physical health are not separate entities, but rather two sides of the same coin. Physical health can have a significant impact on mental health, and vice versa. The following are some of the key ways that physical health and mental health are linked:

Physical health problems can cause mental health problems: Individuals who are dealing with physical health problems, such as chronic pain or a serious illness, are at an increased risk of developing mental health problems, such as depression or anxiety.

Mental health problems can cause physical health problems: Conversely, individuals who are struggling with mental health issues may be more likely to develop physical health problems, such as heart disease or diabetes, as a result of unhealthy behaviors or lifestyle choices.

Lifestyle factors can impact both physical and mental health: Lifestyle factors such as diet, exercise, sleep, and stress management can have a significant impact on both physical and mental health.

Evidence Supporting the Mind-Body Connection

The mind-body connection is supported by a growing body of scientific research. The following are some of the key findings from this research:

Exercise can improve mental health: Regular exercise has been shown to be an effective treatment for depression and anxiety, and can also improve self-esteem and cognitive function.

Nutrition can impact mental health: A diet high in processed foods and refined sugars has been linked to an increased risk of depression and other mental health problems, while a diet rich in fruits, vegetables, and other nutrient-dense foods has been shown to have a protective effect.

Sleep is critical for mental health: Chronic sleep deprivation has been linked to an increased risk of depression, anxiety, and other mental health problems, while getting enough quality sleep can have a positive impact on mood, memory, and cognitive function.

Implications for Individuals and Society

Understanding the link between physical health and mental health has important implications for both individuals and society as a whole. The following are some of the key implications:

Individuals can take steps to improve their mental health by focusing on their physical health: By making lifestyle changes such as exercising regularly, eating a healthy diet, and getting enough sleep, individuals can improve their mental health and overall well-being.

Addressing mental health issues can have positive impacts on physical health: Treating mental health problems can have positive effects on physical health, such as reducing the risk of heart disease and other chronic illnesses.

Addressing the mind-body connection can have significant societal impacts: By recognizing and addressing the link between physical and mental health, society can work to reduce the burden of chronic disease and mental health problems, improving the health and well-being of individuals and communities.

Conclusion

The link between physical health and mental health is clear, with the evidence supporting this connection growing every day. By recognizing this link, individuals can take steps to improve their mental health by focusing on their physical health, and society can work to reduce the burden of chronic disease and mental health problems. In the chapters that follow, we will explore this link in greater detail, discussing the specific ways in which physical health can impact mental health, and how individuals can take steps to improve both.

Have you ever noticed how you feel mentally after a good workout or a healthy meal? Or perhaps you've noticed how your mood can be negatively affected by physical ailments like chronic pain or illness. The mind-body connection is a complex and intricate system that has fascinated scientists and philosophers for centuries. In this chapter, we'll take a closer look at how physical health affects mental health and explore the scientific research that supports this connection.

The Science of the Mind-Body Connection

The mind-body connection is the idea that our physical health is closely linked to our mental and emotional well-being. This connection has been studied extensively by researchers in fields like psychology, neuroscience, and medicine. While the connection may seem intuitive to some, the scientific evidence supporting it is robust and compelling.

The Role of Neurotransmitters

One of the key ways that physical health affects mental health is through the release of neurotransmitters in the brain. These chemicals act as messengers between nerve cells and can have a powerful impact on our mood, emotions, and behavior. For example, the neurotransmitter serotonin is closely linked to feelings of happiness and well-being. Low levels of serotonin have been linked to depression and anxiety disorders.

The Immune System and Mental Health

The immune system is another important player in the mind-body connection. Research has shown that chronic inflammation, which can be caused by a variety of physical health problems, can lead to changes in the brain that can increase the risk of mental health disorders like depression and anxiety. Additionally, the stress hormones released during an immune response can have negative effects on mental health if they are not properly regulated.

The Gut-Brain Axis

The gut-brain axis is another area of research that has gained significant attention in recent years. This connection refers to the complex communication system between the gut and the brain. The gut is home to millions of bacteria that play an important role in digestion and overall health. However, these bacteria also have a significant impact on mental health. Research has shown that changes in the gut microbiome can lead to changes in mood and behavior, and can even increase the risk of mental health disorders.

The Impact of Physical Health on Mental Health

So, we know that physical health can affect mental health, but how exactly does this impact our day-to-day lives? Let's take a closer look.

Depression and Anxiety

Depression and anxiety are two of the most common mental health disorders in the world. While there are many factors that contribute to these disorders, research has shown that physical health is a key player. For example, chronic pain or illness can significantly increase the risk of developing depression or anxiety. Additionally, the release of stress hormones during periods of physical stress can exacerbate these disorders.

Cognitive Function

Physical health also has a significant impact on cognitive function. Research has shown that regular exercise can improve memory, attention, and other cognitive abilities. Additionally, a healthy diet that is rich in nutrients can also boost cognitive function. On the other hand, physical health problems like chronic pain or illness can have a negative impact on cognitive function, making it more difficult to focus or remember important information.

Substance Abuse

Substance abuse is another area where physical health can impact mental health. For example, chronic pain or illness can increase the risk of developing a substance use disorder. Additionally, substance abuse can have negative effects on physical health, which can in turn lead to mental health problems.

Conclusion

The mind-body connection is a fascinating and complex system that has been studied extensively by scientists in a variety of fields. The evidence supporting the connection between physical health and mental health is robust and compelling. From neurotransmitter activity in the brain to inflammation levels in the body, there are many physiological mechanisms that explain how physical health affects mental health. Let's explore some of the key findings from scientific research on this topic:

Neurotransmitters

Neurotransmitters are chemical messengers in the brain that transmit signals between neurons. They play a crucial role in regulating mood, behavior, and cognition. Research has shown that exercise and other forms of physical activity can increase the production of neurotransmitters like dopamine, serotonin, and norepinephrine. These chemicals are associated with positive mood states, and their increased levels in the brain are linked to lower rates of depression and anxiety.

Inflammation

Inflammation is a natural response of the immune system to infection or injury. However, chronic inflammation can have negative effects on physical and mental health. Studies have found that people with depression and anxiety have higher levels of inflammation in their bodies compared to people without these conditions. This link between inflammation and mental health suggests that reducing inflammation through lifestyle changes, such as exercise and diet, may have positive effects on mental well-being.

Stress

Stress is a normal part of life, but chronic stress can have negative effects on both physical and mental health. Chronic stress is associated with increased levels of cortisol, a hormone that plays a role in regulating stress responses. Research has shown that cortisol levels can be lowered through exercise and other forms of physical activity. Additionally, studies have found that regular exercise can reduce symptoms of depression and anxiety in people who are chronically stressed.

Sleep

Sleep is essential for physical and mental health, and lack of sleep has been linked to a range of health problems, including depression and anxiety. Research has shown that exercise can improve sleep quality and duration, which can have positive effects on mental health. Additionally, studies have found that regular exercise can reduce symptoms of insomnia and improve overall sleep quality.

Brain structure and function

Research has shown that physical activity can have positive effects on brain structure and function. For example, studies have found that exercise can increase the volume of gray matter in the brain, which is associated with improved cognitive function. Additionally, research has shown that exercise can improve connectivity between different regions of the brain, which is linked to improved cognitive function and reduced risk of depression.

Overall, the scientific research on how physical health affects mental health is robust and compelling. By understanding the mechanisms behind the mind-body connection, we can make informed decisions about how to improve our physical and mental well-being.

Journal Exercises

Reflect on your current physical health habits. Write about your typical diet, exercise routine, sleep patterns, and self-care practices. How do you feel physically and mentally on a day-to-day basis? Are there any changes you could make to improve your physical health and potentially enhance your mental health?

_____
_____
_____
_____
_____
_____
_____
_____
_____
_____
_____
_____

Write about a time when you noticed a connection between your physical health and mental health. For example, maybe you were going through a stressful period in your life and found that exercising helped you manage your anxiety. Or maybe you experienced a physical health issue that impacted your mental well-being. Reflect on how these experiences shaped your understanding of the mind-body connection.

Take a few minutes to do a body scan. Close your eyes and bring your attention to each part of your body, starting at the top of your head and working your way down to your toes. Notice any areas of tension or discomfort, as well as any areas that feel relaxed and comfortable. Write about your experience and reflect on how this exercise made you feel.

_____
_____
_____
_____
_____
_____
_____
_____
_____
_____
_____
_____
_____
_____
_____
_____
_____
_____
_____

Write about a time when you struggled with managing your emotions. How did you cope with these challenges?

_____
_____
_____

Did you try any physical health strategies, such as exercise or sleep, to help regulate your emotions? If so, how effective were these strategies?

Reflect on the role of social support in the link between physical health and mental health. Write about a time when you received support from someone else during a challenging time. How did this support impact your mental and physical well-being?

How do you typically seek out social support when you need it?

Personal Survey

Do you believe there is a connection between physical health and mental health?
Yes
No
Not sure

Have you ever experienced improvements in your mental health as a result of improving your physical health (e.g., exercising more, eating healthier)?
Yes
No
Not sure

Have you ever experienced declines in your mental health as a result of declines in your physical health (e.g., being sick or injured, not exercising regularly)?
Yes
No
Not sure

How frequently do you engage in physical activity (e.g., exercising, walking, biking)?
Every day
A few times a week
A few times a month
Rarely or never

How would you rate your overall mental health?
Excellent
Good
Fair
Poor

How would you rate your overall physical health?

Excellent
Good
Fair
Poor

Do you believe that mental health should be a priority in overall health and wellness?
Yes
No
Not sure

Are you aware of any resources or support available to help improve your mental health through physical health practices (e.g., exercise programs, healthy eating resources)?
Yes
No
Not sure

Have you ever discussed the link between physical health and mental health with a healthcare provider (e.g., doctor, therapist)?
Yes
No
Not applicable

How important do you believe it is to prioritize both physical and mental health in overall wellness?
Extremely important
Somewhat important
Not very important
Not at all important

Quiz

What is the term used to describe the communication system between the brain and the body?
A) Mind-body connection
B) Neurotransmission
C) Central nervous system
D) Peripheral nervous system

Which of the following is an example of a physical activity that can positively impact mental health?
A) Watching TV
B) Playing video games
C) Jogging
D) Eating junk food

What is the name of the hormone released during exercise that is known to improve mood and reduce stress?
A) Serotonin
B) Endorphins
C) Dopamine
D) Cortisol

Which of the following is NOT a benefit of getting enough sleep for mental health?
A) Improved memory and concentration
B) Reduced risk of depression and anxiety
C) Increased likelihood of weight gain
D) Improved emotional regulation

True or False: Chronic stress can have negative effects on both physical and mental health.
A) True
B) False

Explanation of the relationship between exercise, diet, sleep, and mental health

It's no secret that exercise, diet, and sleep are all essential for maintaining good physical health. But did you know that these factors also play a crucial role in our mental health and well-being? In this chapter, we will explore the connection between exercise, diet, sleep, and mental health, and how they can impact each other. We will examine the scientific research on this topic and discuss practical tips for incorporating healthy habits into our daily lives.

Exercise and Mental Health:

Regular exercise has been shown to have numerous benefits for mental health. Studies have found that physical activity can help reduce symptoms of depression and anxiety, as well as improve overall mood and well-being. Exercise has also been linked to increased brain function and better cognitive performance. One theory is that exercise increases the production of endorphins, which are chemicals in the brain that are associated with feelings of happiness and euphoria.

Diet and Mental Health:

The foods we eat can also have a significant impact on our mental health. A balanced and nutritious diet can help improve mood, energy levels, and overall well-being. On the other hand, a diet high in sugar and processed foods has been linked to an increased risk of depression and anxiety. Research has also shown that certain nutrients, such as omega-3 fatty acids, can be particularly beneficial for mental health.

Sleep and Mental Health:

Getting enough quality sleep is essential for both physical and mental health. Sleep deprivation has been linked to a range of mental health issues, including depression, anxiety, and mood disorders. Lack of sleep can also impair cognitive function and make it more difficult to regulate emotions. On the other hand, getting enough sleep can help improve mood, memory, and overall cognitive performance.

The Interconnectedness of Exercise, Diet, and Sleep:
While each of these factors on its own can have a significant impact on mental health, they are also interconnected. For example, regular exercise can help improve sleep quality, which in turn can lead to better mental health outcomes. Similarly, a healthy diet can provide the nutrients and energy needed for physical activity, while also promoting better sleep. It's important to consider all of these factors together when trying to improve mental health and well-being.

Practical Tips for Improving Mental Health:
Incorporating healthy habits into our daily lives can help improve mental health and well-being. Some practical tips include:

- ❖ Engage in regular physical activity, such as going for a walk, bike ride, or taking a fitness class.
- ❖ Eat a balanced and nutritious diet that includes plenty of fruits, vegetables, whole grains, and lean proteins.
- ❖ Prioritize getting enough sleep each night, aiming for 7-9 hours of quality sleep.
- ❖ Practice stress-reducing techniques, such as meditation, deep breathing, or yoga.
- ❖ Seek professional help if experiencing persistent mental health issues, such as depression or anxiety.

Conclusion:
The relationship between exercise, diet, sleep, and mental health is a complex and multifaceted one. By understanding this connection and taking steps to prioritize healthy habits, we can improve our overall

well-being and promote better mental health outcomes. Remember, small changes can add up to make a big difference.

Physical health and mental health are closely intertwined, and many studies have shown that improving physical health can have a positive impact on mental health. In this chapter, we will explore some examples of individuals who have improved their mental health by making changes to their physical health habits.

Examples of People who Improved their Mental Health:

Jane:
Jane had struggled with anxiety and depression for years. She tried therapy and medication, but nothing seemed to work. One day, she decided to try running as a way to get in shape. She found that running not only helped her lose weight and get in shape but also helped reduce her anxiety and depression symptoms. She started to run regularly, and as she improved her physical health, her mental health improved as well.

Tom:
Tom had been struggling with sleep issues for years. He would often wake up feeling tired and groggy, which would affect his mood and productivity throughout the day. He started to focus on his sleep habits by going to bed and waking up at the same time every day, creating a relaxing bedtime routine, and avoiding caffeine and alcohol before bed. As he improved his sleep, he found that his mood and energy levels improved as well.

Sarah:
Sarah had a history of binge eating and had struggled with her weight for years. She decided to start working with a nutritionist and focused on improving her diet by eating more whole foods and reducing processed and sugary foods. As she started to lose weight and

improve her physical health, she found that her self-esteem and confidence improved, and she felt better about herself overall.

Conclusion:

These are just a few examples of how improving physical health can have a positive impact on mental health. It is essential to remember that everyone's journey to improving their physical and mental health is different. However, making small changes to our physical health habits can have a significant impact on our mental health and well-being.

CHAPTER 2: EXERCISE AND MENTAL HEALTH

Physical exercise is essential to maintain good health and overall well-being. However, did you know that exercise can also have a significant impact on your mental health? The benefits of exercise go beyond the physical changes that you see in your body. Regular exercise has been shown to have a positive impact on your mood, cognitive function, and overall mental health. In this chapter, we will explore the relationship between exercise and mental health and provide you with the tools you need to make exercise a regular part of your mental health routine.

The Benefits of Exercise on Mental Health

Physical exercise has been shown to have numerous benefits on mental health. Some of the benefits of exercise on mental health include:

Reducing Symptoms of Depression and Anxiety
Exercise has been shown to be an effective tool in reducing symptoms of depression and anxiety. Studies have shown that exercise can be just as effective as medication in treating mild to moderate depression and anxiety.

Boosting Mood

Regular exercise has been shown to increase the production of endorphins, which are the body's natural mood-boosting chemicals. This increase in endorphins can result in a decrease in feelings of anxiety, depression, and stress.

Improving Cognitive Function

Exercise has been shown to have a positive impact on cognitive function. Regular exercise has been linked to improved memory, attention, and decision-making skills.

Reducing Stress

Exercise can be an effective tool in reducing stress. Regular exercise has been shown to decrease the production of stress hormones such as cortisol and adrenaline.

Improving Sleep

Exercise has been shown to improve sleep quality, which is essential for good mental health. Studies have shown that people who exercise regularly fall asleep faster, stay asleep longer, and wake up feeling more rested.

Examples of People Who Improved Their Mental Health by Improving Their Physical Health

Sarah

Sarah was a single mother who had been struggling with depression and anxiety for years. She found it difficult to motivate herself to exercise, but eventually, she decided to start small by taking a walk every day. Over time, Sarah gradually increased the length of her walks and started to incorporate other forms of exercise into her routine, such as yoga and weightlifting. Sarah noticed a significant improvement in her mood and overall mental health. She was less anxious and depressed and felt more energized and confident.

Michael

Michael had been dealing with stress and burnout at work for years. He found it challenging to find time to exercise regularly, but he knew that he needed to make a change. Michael started by taking a 20-minute walk during his lunch break every day. Over time, Michael increased the intensity of his workouts and started to incorporate more strength training into his routine. Michael noticed that he had more energy throughout the day, was less stressed, and was able to focus better at work.

Amanda

Amanda had been dealing with chronic insomnia for years. She had tried medication, meditation, and other remedies, but nothing seemed to work. Amanda decided to try incorporating regular exercise into her routine. She started by doing gentle yoga every morning and gradually increased the intensity of her workouts over time. Amanda noticed a significant improvement in her sleep quality. She was falling asleep faster, staying asleep longer, and waking up feeling more rested and energized.

Conclusion

In conclusion, exercise is a powerful tool that can have a significant impact on your mental health. Whether you are struggling with depression, anxiety, stress, or simply want to improve your overall well-being, regular exercise can help. By incorporating exercise into your daily routine, you can experience the numerous benefits that exercise has on your mental health. So why not give it a try? Start small, set achievable goals, and watch as exercise transforms your mental health and your

The mental health benefits of exercise, including reduced stress and anxiety

We all know that exercise is good for our physical health, but did you know that it also has many mental health benefits? In this chapter, we will explore the ways that exercise can improve our mental well-being, including reducing stress and anxiety. We will delve into the scientific research behind this and provide you with practical tips for incorporating exercise into your daily routine.

The Mental Health Benefits of Exercise:

Exercise has been shown to have numerous benefits for our mental health. Here are some of the ways in which exercise can positively impact our mental well-being:

Reduces Stress:

Exercise is an excellent way to reduce stress. When we exercise, our body releases endorphins, which are natural chemicals that make us feel good. These endorphins help to counteract the negative effects of stress and promote feelings of calm and relaxation. Additionally, exercise can provide a healthy outlet for pent-up stress and anxiety.

Reduces Anxiety:

Exercise has also been shown to reduce symptoms of anxiety. In fact, studies have found that regular exercise can be just as effective as medication for treating anxiety disorders. Exercise helps to reduce anxiety by increasing the production of neurotransmitters like serotonin and norepinephrine, which can improve mood and decrease feelings of fear and anxiety.

Improves Mood:

Exercise can also help to improve our overall mood. As mentioned, exercise releases endorphins, which can make us feel good. Additionally, exercise can help to boost our self-confidence and self-esteem, which can have a positive impact on our mood.

Improves Sleep:

Exercise can also improve the quality of our sleep. Research has shown that regular exercise can help to improve the duration and quality of sleep, which can have a significant impact on our mental well-being.

Boosts Brain Function:

Exercise has been shown to boost brain function by improving cognitive abilities like memory, attention, and processing speed. Exercise increases blood flow to the brain, which helps to nourish brain cells and promote the growth of new ones.

The Science Behind Exercise and Mental Health:

So, how exactly does exercise have these mental health benefits? The answer lies in the complex interplay between our brain and body. Exercise affects our brain in many ways, including:

Neurotransmitters:

As mentioned, exercise increases the production of neurotransmitters like serotonin and norepinephrine, which can improve mood and reduce anxiety.

Brain-Derived Neurotrophic Factor (BDNF):

Exercise also increases the production of a protein called BDNF, which promotes the growth of new neurons in the brain. This can improve cognitive function and help to protect against cognitive decline.

Hippocampus:

Exercise has been shown to increase the size of the hippocampus, which is a part of the brain that is important for memory and learning. This can help to improve cognitive function and reduce the risk of age-related cognitive decline.

Stress Response:

Exercise can also help to improve our body's stress response. Regular exercise can help to decrease the production of stress hormones like cortisol and adrenaline, which can have negative effects on our mental and physical health.

Tips for Incorporating Exercise into Your Routine:

Now that we know how important exercise is for our mental health, here are some tips for incorporating exercise into your daily routine:

Start Small:

If you're new to exercise, start small and gradually build up. Even just a few minutes of exercise per day can have a positive impact on your mental health.

Find an Activity You Enjoy:

Choose an activity that you enjoy so that exercise doesn't feel like a chore. Whether it's hiking, swimming, or dancing, there are many different ways to get moving and have fun at the same time.

Make it a Habit:

Try to make exercise a regular part of your routine, just like brushing your teeth or taking a shower. This can help you establish a habit and make it easier to stick to over time. Start with small goals, such as 10 minutes of physical activity a day, and gradually increase the duration and intensity of your workouts as your fitness level improves.

It's important to find an exercise routine that you enjoy and that fits your lifestyle. This will make it more likely that you'll stick with it long-term. If you don't like going to the gym, try outdoor activities like hiking or biking, or at-home workouts like yoga or bodyweight exercises. The key is to find something that you find fun and engaging, so that exercise becomes something that you look forward to rather than dread.

One of the most important things to keep in mind when it comes to exercise and mental health is that it's not about achieving a certain body type or reaching a specific weight. Exercise should be seen as a tool for improving your overall well-being, both physically and mentally. So don't get discouraged if you don't see immediate changes in your body composition - focus on the positive impact that exercise is having on your mental health.

The Science Behind Exercise and Mental Health
There is a growing body of research that supports the idea that exercise can have a positive impact on mental health. Here are just a few of the ways that exercise can benefit your mental well-being:

Reduced Stress and Anxiety

One of the most well-known benefits of exercise is its ability to reduce stress and anxiety. Exercise triggers the release of endorphins, which are natural chemicals that help to reduce stress and improve mood. It also helps to reduce the levels of cortisol, a stress hormone, in the body.

Several studies have shown that regular exercise can reduce symptoms of anxiety and depression, as well as improve overall mood. In one study, for example, researchers found that just 30 minutes of exercise a day was enough to significantly reduce symptoms of anxiety and depression in participants.

Improved Cognitive Function

Exercise has also been shown to have a positive impact on cognitive function. This includes things like memory, attention, and processing speed. One study found that just 20 minutes of moderate exercise was enough to improve cognitive function in participants.

Better Sleep

Exercise can also help to improve sleep quality, which is important for mental health. Regular exercise has been shown to help people fall asleep faster, stay asleep longer, and experience better quality sleep overall.

Boosted Self-Esteem

Regular exercise can also improve self-esteem and body image, which are important factors in overall mental health. Exercise can help you feel better about your body and your abilities, which can translate into greater confidence in other areas of your life.

Conclusion

In conclusion, exercise can have a powerful impact on mental health. By reducing stress and anxiety, improving cognitive function, and boosting self-esteem, exercise can help you feel better both physically and mentally. So if you're looking for a natural and effective way to improve your mental well-being, start incorporating exercise into your daily routine today. Remember, it's not about achieving a certain body type or reaching a specific weight - it's about using exercise as a tool for improving your overall well-being.

Journal exercises
Reflect on your own experiences with exercise and mental health. Have you noticed any changes in your mood or stress levels after working out? How do you feel mentally when you skip a workout?

_____
_____
_____
_____
_____
_____
_____
_____
_____
_____
_____
_____
_____
_____
_____
_____
_____
_____

Consider your current exercise routine. Are there any changes you could make to prioritize your mental health?

___

For example, could you incorporate more mindfulness practices into your workout or switch up your routine to prevent boredom?

___

Write about any barriers or obstacles that prevent you from exercising regularly. Are there ways to overcome these challenges or work around them?

Think about the types of exercise you enjoy and how you can incorporate them into your routine. If you don't enjoy traditional workouts, are there other physical activities you could do that would still provide mental health benefits?

Journal about your favorite outdoor places to exercise and how being in nature affects your mental health. Do you notice a difference in your mood when you work out outside versus indoors?

_____
_____
_____
_____
_____
_____
_____
_____
_____
_____
_____
_____
_____
_____
_____
_____
_____
_____
_____

Consider any social aspects of exercise that might contribute to your mental health. Do you prefer to work out alone or with others?

_____
_____
_____
_____
_____
_____

How does the social component of exercise impact your mood and motivation?

_____
_____
_____
_____

Write about any exercise-related goals you have and how achieving them could benefit your mental health. For example, if you want to run a 5K, how might that boost your self-confidence and mood?

_____
_____
_____
_____
_____
_____
_____
_____
_____
_____
_____
_____
_____
_____
_____
_____

Think about how you can track your exercise progress in a way that motivates you. Do you prefer to use an app or journal your workouts?

_____

How can you celebrate your accomplishments along the way?

Write about any past negative experiences with exercise and how they might be holding you back from prioritizing your mental health through physical activity. Are there ways to reframe these experiences in a more positive light?

Finally, consider how you can integrate exercise into your daily life in a way that is sustainable and enjoyable. How can you make it a habit and prioritize your mental health through physical activity in the long-term?

Quiz

What are some mental health benefits of exercise?
A) Increased stress and anxiety
B) Decreased stress and anxiety
C) Increased depression and mood swings
D) Decreased depression and mood swings

What is one way exercise can reduce stress?
A) By increasing cortisol levels
B) By decreasing cortisol levels
C) By increasing adrenaline levels
D) By decreasing adrenaline levels

How often should you exercise to see the mental health benefits?
A) Once a week
B) Twice a week
C) Three times a week
D) At least four times a week

What type of exercise is best for reducing anxiety?
A) Cardiovascular exercise
B) Strength training
C) Yoga
D) High-intensity interval training

What type of exercise can help with depression?
A) Yoga
B) Strength training
C) Cardiovascular exercise
D) High-intensity interval training

How can exercise help improve self-esteem?
A) By making you more self-critical
B) By increasing negative self-talk
C) By helping you achieve fitness goals

D) By increasing feelings of inadequacy

What are some social benefits of exercising with others?
A) Increased isolation and loneliness
B) Increased feelings of belonging and connection
C) Increased competition and hostility
D) Increased feelings of exclusion and rejection

How can you incorporate exercise into your daily routine?
A) By setting small, achievable goals
B) By expecting immediate results
C) By overexerting yourself
D) By neglecting rest and recovery

How can exercise benefit the brain?
A) By decreasing blood flow to the brain
B) By decreasing neuroplasticity
C) By increasing neuroplasticity
D) By decreasing the production of brain-derived neurotrophic factor (BDNF)

What is the key to making exercise a habit?
A) Consistency
B) Intensity
C) Variety
D) Perfectionism

Making Time for Exercise in a Busy Life

In today's fast-paced world, we often find ourselves caught up in the hustle and bustle of work, family, and social obligations. As a result, it can be challenging to make time for exercise, despite the numerous physical and mental health benefits it provides. However, with some creativity and a bit of planning, it's possible to incorporate exercise into even the busiest of lifestyles.

In this chapter, we will explore some tips and strategies for making exercise a regular part of your routine, even when you have a hectic schedule. From quick and efficient workouts to creative ways to sneak in activity throughout the day, we'll provide you with the tools you need to prioritize your health and fitness.

Identifying Barriers to Exercise

Before we dive into strategies for incorporating exercise into a busy lifestyle, it's essential to identify any potential barriers that may be preventing you from working out. These could include:

Lack of time
Lack of motivation
Feeling overwhelmed or stressed
Physical limitations or injuries
By identifying these barriers, you can begin to develop strategies to overcome them and make exercise a regular part of your routine.

Quick and Efficient Workouts

When time is tight, it's essential to have a few go-to workouts that you can complete in a short amount of time. Here are some ideas:

HIIT (High-Intensity Interval Training) - This involves alternating periods of high-intensity exercise with periods of rest or low-intensity exercise. These workouts can be completed in as little as 15-20 minutes and provide a significant cardiovascular and strength-training workout.
Tabata - Similar to HIIT, Tabata involves 20 seconds of high-intensity exercise followed by 10 seconds of rest, repeated for four minutes. This method can be used with a variety of exercises, including bodyweight exercises, kettlebell swings, and cycling.
Circuit Training - A circuit is a series of exercises completed in succession with little to no rest between them. This type of workout can be done with bodyweight exercises or with weights, and can be completed in as little as 20-30 minutes.

Section 3: Sneaking in Exercise Throughout the Day

Another way to make exercise a regular part of your routine is to sneak in activity throughout the day. Here are some ideas:

Take the Stairs - Whenever possible, take the stairs instead of the elevator. This provides an excellent cardiovascular workout and helps strengthen the muscles in your legs.

Walk or Bike to Work - If you live close enough to work, consider walking or biking instead of driving. This is an excellent way to get some fresh air and exercise, and it can also help you save money on gas and parking.

Stand Up and Stretch - If you work at a desk job, make sure to stand up and stretch every 30-60 minutes. This can help reduce back pain and improve circulation.

Section 4: Prioritizing Exercise

One of the most important things you can do to make exercise a regular part of your routine is to prioritize it. Here are some tips:

Schedule It - Just like you would schedule a meeting or appointment, schedule your workouts into your calendar. This helps ensure that you set aside the time and don't let other obligations get in the way.

Make It a Habit - As we discussed earlier, making exercise a habit can help make it easier to stick with over the long-term. Find a time that works for you, and make it a regular part of your routine.

Find a Workout Buddy - Having a workout partner can help keep you accountable and make exercise more enjoyable. Consider finding a friend or family member to work out with regularly.

Conclusion

Incorporating exercise into a busy lifestyle Incorporating exercise into a busy lifestyle can be challenging, but it is not impossible. With the right mindset, planning, and commitment, anyone can make exercise a part of their daily routine. The benefits of regular exercise are numerous, including improved physical and mental health, increased energy levels, and reduced stress and anxiety. So, if you are struggling to find time for exercise, remember that it is not a luxury, but a necessity for a healthy and happy life.

Tips for Incorporating Exercise into a Busy Lifestyle:

Start small: Don't try to do too much too soon. Start with short exercise sessions and gradually increase the duration and intensity.

Make a plan: Schedule your exercise sessions just like you would schedule a meeting or appointment. Make it a non-negotiable part of your day.

Be flexible: If your schedule gets hectic, adjust your exercise routine accordingly. Even a few minutes of activity can make a difference.

Find an accountability partner: Working out with a friend or joining a fitness group can help you stay motivated and committed.

Make use of technology: Use apps or fitness trackers to monitor your progress and set goals.

Incorporate exercise into your daily routine: Walk or bike to work, take the stairs instead of the elevator, or do a few simple exercises while watching TV.

Get creative: Find ways to make exercise fun and enjoyable. Try new activities, listen to music, or watch your favorite TV show while working out.

Prioritize self-care: Remember that exercise is not just about physical health, but also mental health. Prioritize your self-care by taking time to relax and recharge.

Reward yourself: Celebrate your accomplishments and milestones with small rewards, such as a new workout outfit or a massage.

Stay positive: Don't be too hard on yourself if you miss a workout or have a setback. Stay positive and focus on the progress you have made.

Incorporating exercise into a busy lifestyle is not easy, but it is worth the effort. By making exercise a priority, you will not only improve your physical health but also your mental and emotional well-being. So, take the first step today and start making exercise a part of your daily routine.

Exercise is not just beneficial for physical health, but also for mental health. Regular exercise has been shown to help reduce stress, anxiety, and depression, and increase self-esteem and overall well-being. In this chapter, we will share inspiring stories of individuals who have improved their mental health through exercise.

Success Stories

Jane's Story
Jane had been struggling with anxiety and depression for years, and was on medication to manage her symptoms. She felt like she was in a constant fog, and had difficulty getting through her day-to-day tasks. One day, she decided to try going for a walk in her local park. She found that the fresh air and movement helped to clear her mind, and she felt a sense of accomplishment after completing her walk. She continued to incorporate daily walks into her routine, gradually increasing the duration and intensity of her exercise. Over time, she was able to wean off her medication, and felt more energized and positive than she had in years.

Tom's Story

Tom had always been an avid runner, but when he experienced a traumatic event, he found that his running became even more important for his mental health. He used running as a way to cope with his emotions and release any pent-up frustration or anger. He found that running not only helped him manage his symptoms of anxiety and depression, but also helped him to feel more confident and empowered.

Maria's Story

Maria had been dealing with work-related stress for years, and had tried a number of different coping strategies without success. One day, she decided to try taking a yoga class. She found that the combination of movement and mindfulness helped to calm her mind and reduce her stress levels. She continued to practice yoga on a regular basis, and found that it not only helped her manage her work-related stress, but also improved her overall mental health and well-being.

Tips for Getting Started

If you're looking to improve your mental health through exercise, here are some tips to help you get started:

Start Small

It's important to set realistic goals for yourself when starting an exercise routine. Start with something small, like a 10-minute walk or a short yoga practice, and gradually increase the duration and intensity of your exercise over time.

Find Something You Enjoy

The key to sticking with an exercise routine is finding something you enjoy. Whether it's running, dancing, or playing a sport, find an activity that you look forward to doing.

Incorporate Exercise into Your Daily Routine

If you're short on time, try to find ways to incorporate exercise into your daily routine. Take the stairs instead of the elevator, or walk or bike to work if possible.

Make it Social

Exercise doesn't have to be a solitary activity. Join a sports team or fitness class, or find a workout buddy to help keep you motivated and accountable.

Conclusion

Exercise is a powerful tool for improving mental health, and the stories of Jane, Tom, and Maria serve as inspiring examples of the transformative power of exercise. By starting small, finding an activity you enjoy, and incorporating exercise into your daily routine, you can improve your mental health and overall well-being. So why not lace up your sneakers and get moving today? Your mind (and body) will thank you.

CHAPTER 3 MENTAL HEALTH AFTER A LIFE-CHANGING EVENT

Examples of individuals who have faced life-changing events and improved their mental health
Discussion of how they coped and what strategies were most effective
Inspirational messages for readers to take away
VI. Conclusion

Recap of key points from the chapter
Final thoughts and encouragement for those struggling with mental health after a life-changing event
Reminder to seek help and support when needed.

Life is unpredictable and can throw us unexpected curveballs. Sometimes, these curveballs can be life-changing events that leave a profound impact on our mental health. Perhaps it's a near-death experience, a physical or mental trauma, or a sudden loss of a loved one. Whatever the event may be, it can leave us feeling lost, overwhelmed, and struggling to cope with our emotions. It's easy to feel like we're stuck in a dark hole with no way out. But it's important to remember that it's possible to find light in the darkness and come out stronger on the other side. In this chapter, we will explore how to navigate the difficult journey of rebuilding your mental health after a life-changing event. We will share strategies, tools, and real-life stories of individuals who have faced similar challenges and come out the other side. With patience, self-compassion, and the right mindset, you too can heal and reclaim your mental wellbeing.

Definition of life-changing events

Life is full of twists and turns, and sometimes those twists can completely alter the course of our lives. These events, whether positive or negative, have the power to change our perspective, our relationships, and even our mental health. They are known as life-changing events, and they can be anything from a near-death experience to a major illness or injury, a divorce, the loss of a loved one, or a big career change.

No matter the cause, a life-changing event can shake our world to the core and leave us feeling lost and unsure of how to move forward. It is during these times that our mental health is most vulnerable, and we may experience symptoms of depression, anxiety, PTSD, or other mental health issues.

But there is hope. With the right mindset, resources, and support, it is possible to overcome the mental health challenges that come with life-changing events and emerge stronger and more resilient than before. In this chapter, we will explore what life-changing events are, how they can impact our mental health, and what steps we can take to navigate these changes and come out the other side stronger and more resilient. So let's dive in!

Defining Life-Changing Events

Life-changing events are events that have a significant impact on our lives, whether positive or negative. These events can be sudden or gradual, and they can happen to anyone, regardless of age, gender, or background. Some examples of life-changing events include:

- A serious illness or injury
- The death of a loved one
- A divorce or breakup
- The loss of a job or major career change
- Moving to a new city or country
- Financial hardship or bankruptcy
- Starting a new business or venture
- Winning the lottery or a major prize

A significant achievement, such as a degree or certification

While some life-changing events are positive, such as starting a new business or winning the lottery, others can be extremely difficult, such as the death of a loved one or a serious illness. Regardless of the nature of the event, all life-changing events have the potential to impact our mental health in significant ways.

The Impact of Life-Changing Events on Mental Health

Life-changing events can cause a wide range of emotional and psychological responses, and these responses can vary widely from person to person. Some common psychological responses to life-changing events include:

- Shock or disbelief
- Anger or resentment
- Sadness or grief

- Anxiety or fear
- Guilt or shame
- Depression or hopelessness
- Post-traumatic stress disorder (PTSD)

These emotional responses can be extremely challenging to deal with, and they can impact our mental health in a number of ways. Some of the potential mental health impacts of life-changing events include:

- Increased stress and anxiety
- Depression and feelings of hopelessness
- Difficulty sleeping or insomnia
- Changes in appetite or weight
- Substance abuse or addiction
- Relationship issues or social isolation
- Chronic pain or physical health problems

It is important to note that everyone responds differently to life-changing events, and some people may be more resilient than others. However, it is important to take steps to support our mental health during these times, regardless of our level of resilience. In the next section, we will explore some tips and strategies for coping with the mental health challenges that come with life-changing events.

Life-changing events and their impact on mental health

Life is full of ups and downs, and sometimes we experience events that have a profound impact on our lives. These events, also known as life-changing events, can range from positive ones like getting married, having a child, or getting a new job, to negative ones like a near-death experience, physical or mental trauma, or the loss of a loved one. While positive life-changing events can bring joy and excitement, negative ones can have a significant impact on our mental health. In this chapter, we'll take a closer look at life-changing events and how they can affect our mental well-being.

What are life-changing events?
Life-changing events can be defined as significant events that alter the course of our lives in some way. These events can be positive or negative and can have a lasting impact on our lives. Some common life-changing events include:

➤ Getting married or divorced

➤ Having a child or adopting a child

➤ Losing a loved one

➤ Being diagnosed with a serious illness

➤ Moving to a new city or country

➤ Starting a new job or losing a job

➤ Retiring from work

➤ Experiencing a natural disaster

➤ Surviving a near-death experience

➤ Being a victim of a crime or abuse

➤ How can life-changing events affect mental health?

Life-changing events can have a significant impact on our mental health. Depending on the nature of the event, it can cause feelings of stress, anxiety, depression, and even post-traumatic stress disorder (PTSD). Here are some ways in which life-changing events can affect our mental health:

Stress and anxiety

Life-changing events can cause significant stress and anxiety, which can have a negative impact on our mental health. For example, if you're going through a divorce or the loss of a loved one, you may experience intense feelings of sadness, anxiety, and stress. These feelings can make it difficult to cope with everyday tasks, and it may even lead to physical symptoms like headaches, stomachaches, and insomnia.

Depression

Depression is a common mental health disorder that can be triggered by a life-changing event. For example, if you lose your job or retire from work, you may experience a sense of loss and purposelessness, which can lead to feelings of depression. Similarly, if you're diagnosed with a serious illness, you may experience depression as a result of the fear and uncertainty that comes with the diagnosis.

Post-traumatic stress disorder (PTSD)

Life-changing events like a near-death experience or being a victim of a crime or abuse can lead to PTSD. PTSD is a mental health disorder that can develop after a traumatic event. Symptoms of PTSD can include flashbacks, nightmares, and intense feelings of fear and anxiety.

Coping with life-changing events

While life-changing events can have a significant impact on our mental health, there are things we can do to cope with these events and improve our mental well-being. Here are some tips for coping with life-changing events:

Seek support

It's important to seek support from friends, family, or a mental health professional if you're struggling to cope with a life-changing event. Talking to someone about your feelings can help you process your emotions and come up with a plan for moving forward.

Practice self-care

Self-care is essential during times of stress and anxiety. Take time to prioritize your physical and mental health by eating well, getting enough sleep, and engaging in activities that bring you joy.

Stay active

Exercise has been shown to be an effective way to improve mental health. Even a short walk or yoga session can help to reduce stress and improve mood.

Consider therapy

Therapy can be an effective way to work through the emotions and challenges that come with a life-changing event. Here are some types of therapy that may be helpful:

Cognitive-behavioral therapy (CBT): This type of therapy focuses on identifying negative thought patterns and behaviors and replacing them with more positive and productive ones. CBT can be particularly helpful for people struggling with anxiety, depression, or post-traumatic stress disorder (PTSD).

Eye Movement Desensitization and Reprocessing (EMDR): This is a specialized form of therapy that is used to treat PTSD and other trauma-related disorders. EMDR works by helping individuals process traumatic memories and experiences in a safe and controlled environment.

Group therapy: Group therapy can be particularly helpful for people who are struggling with feelings of isolation or loneliness following a life-changing event. Being able to connect with others who have gone through similar experiences can help individuals feel less alone and more understood.

Mindfulness-based therapies: Mindfulness-based therapies, such as mindfulness-based stress reduction (MBSR) and mindfulness-based cognitive therapy (MBCT), can be helpful for individuals who are struggling with anxiety, depression, or other mental health concerns. These therapies focus on helping individuals develop a greater awareness of their thoughts and emotions, which can help them better manage stress and improve their overall mental health.

It's important to note that therapy is not a one-size-fits-all solution, and what works for one person may not work for another. It may take some trial and error to find the right therapist or type of therapy that works best for you.

Self-care practices

In addition to seeking therapy, there are several self-care practices that can help individuals cope with the emotional aftermath of a life-changing event. Here are some self-care practices to consider:

Exercise: Exercise is a great way to improve mood and reduce stress. Even a short walk outside or a few minutes of stretching can make a big difference.

Mindfulness meditation: Mindfulness meditation can help individuals reduce stress, improve mood, and develop greater self-awareness. It involves focusing on the present moment and paying attention to one's thoughts and emotions without judgment.

Creative expression: Engaging in creative activities, such as writing, drawing, or painting, can be a great way to process emotions and gain a greater sense of control over one's thoughts and feelings.

Social support: Having a support system of family, friends, or a support group can be a crucial component of healing and recovery after a life-changing event. It's important to reach out for help when needed and not to isolate oneself.

Self-compassion: It's important to be kind to oneself during difficult times. Practicing self-compassion involves treating oneself with the same kindness and understanding one would offer to a close friend who is going through a difficult time.

Conclusion

Life-changing events can be incredibly difficult to navigate, and it's normal to experience a range of emotions in their aftermath. However, it's important to remember that there are many resources and strategies available to help individuals cope and move forward. Seeking therapy, practicing self-care, and connecting with supportive individuals can all be powerful tools for healing and growth. With time and support, it is possible to emerge from a life-changing event with greater strength, resilience, and appreciation for life.

Overview of the chapter

Life-changing events can have a significant impact on a person's mental health. This chapter aims to provide an in-depth understanding of the various ways in which life-changing events can affect mental health, and also explores coping strategies to help individuals manage and overcome the challenges they face. The chapter begins with an overview of the different types of life-changing events and their emotional and physical impact. It then delves into the common psychological reactions to such events and emphasizes the importance of seeking professional help.

The next section explores various coping strategies, including self-care techniques such as exercise, healthy eating, and sleep. It also discusses mindfulness practices and meditation, the importance of connecting with supportive friends and family members, and the option of joining support groups or seeking professional counseling. The chapter then explores ways in which individuals can move forward and thrive after a life-changing event. This includes developing resilience, setting realistic goals, finding purpose and meaning, and celebrating progress.

To provide readers with practical insight and inspiration, the chapter includes case studies of individuals who have faced life-changing events and improved their mental health. These stories illustrate how people cope and what strategies were most effective. Finally, the chapter concludes with a recap of key points and a reminder to seek help and support when needed, along with some final thoughts and encouragement for those struggling with mental health after a life-changing event.

Understanding the Impact of Life-Changing Events

Life is unpredictable, and sometimes we face events that can completely transform our existence. These events can come in many forms, such as a serious illness, a traumatic experience, the loss of a loved one, or a major life transition. While some events can be positive and lead to growth and personal development, others can be incredibly challenging and can leave lasting emotional scars. It is important to understand the impact that life-changing events can have on our mental health, as this can help us take the necessary steps to heal and move forward.

Life-changing events can be broadly categorized into three types: expected, unexpected, and transitional.

Expected life-changing events are those that we know are coming and can prepare for, such as retirement, childbirth, or a planned surgery. These events can still be challenging, but having some level of control and preparation can make them more manageable.

Unexpected life-changing events are those that catch us off guard and can be incredibly traumatic, such as a car accident, a natural disaster, or the sudden death of a loved one. These events can cause feelings of shock, disbelief, and intense grief.

Transitional life-changing events are those that involve a major change in our life circumstances, such as a divorce, a move to a new city, or a job loss. While not always traumatic in the same way as unexpected events, they can still be very difficult to navigate and can lead to feelings of uncertainty and anxiety.

The Physical and Emotional Impact of Life-Changing Events

Life-changing events can have both physical and emotional effects on our bodies and minds. Some common physical symptoms include:

- Fatigue
- Insomnia or other sleep disturbances
- Changes in appetite or weight
- Headaches
- Stomach upset or digestive issues
- Muscle tension or pain
- Increased heart rate or blood pressure
- Weakened immune system

Journal Exercises:

Write about a life-changing event that you have experienced. How did it impact you physically and emotionally?

_____
_____
_____
_____
_____
_____
_____
_____

_____
_____
_____
_____
_____
_____
_____
_____
_____
_____

Reflect on the common psychological reactions to life-changing events mentioned in the chapter. Which ones have you experienced and how did you cope with them?

_____
_____
_____
_____
_____
_____
_____
_____
_____
_____
_____
_____
_____
_____

Describe some self-care techniques that have worked for you in the past. How can you incorporate these techniques into your daily routine?

Write about a time when you felt resilient and bounced back after adversity. What strategies did you use to overcome the challenges you faced?

Think about your goals and aspirations for the future. How has your life-changing event impacted these goals, and how can you work towards achieving them?

_____
_____
_____
_____
_____
_____
_____

Survey Questions:

Have you experienced a life-changing event in the past year?

How would you rate the impact of this event on your mental health?

Have you sought professional help or counseling to cope with the event?

Which coping strategies have been most effective for you?

Do you feel that you have developed resilience and grown from the experience?

Quiz Questions:

What are some common psychological reactions to life-changing events?

True or false: Seeking professional help is important for coping with the impact of life-changing events on mental health.

Which self-care techniques can help improve mental health after a life-changing event?

What are some strategies for developing resilience after adversity?

What is the importance of setting realistic goals after a life-changing event?

III. Coping Strategies for Mental Health after a Life-Changing Event

After experiencing a life-changing event, it is not uncommon to feel overwhelmed, lost, and unsure of how to move forward. Coping with the emotional aftermath of such an event can be a challenge, but it is possible to regain a sense of control and find ways to manage your mental health. In this chapter, we will explore various coping strategies to help you navigate the difficult emotions that can arise after a life-changing event. From self-care techniques to mindfulness practices and seeking professional help, we will provide practical tips and tools to help you build resilience and move forward in a positive direction. Remember, it is never too late to take steps towards healing and finding a sense of balance in your life.

Self-care techniques, including exercise, healthy eating, and sleep

Self-care is the act of taking care of oneself physically, mentally, and emotionally. It is a necessary practice for everyone, but especially important for those who have experienced life-changing events that have impacted their mental health. In this chapter, we will explore the importance of self-care for mental health after a life-changing event, and discuss specific techniques such as exercise, healthy eating, and sleep that can help improve mental wellness.

Exercise

Exercise is not only beneficial for physical health, but also for mental health. Regular exercise can improve mood, reduce anxiety and depression, and increase self-esteem. It is important to find a form of exercise that is enjoyable and sustainable, as consistency is key to reaping the benefits. In this section, we will explore different types of exercise, their mental health benefits, and tips for incorporating exercise into daily life.

Healthy Eating

Eating a balanced and nutritious diet is crucial for overall health, including mental health. Certain nutrients, such as omega-3 fatty acids and B vitamins, have been linked to improved mental health outcomes. Additionally, making healthy food choices can improve energy levels, reduce stress, and boost mood. In this section, we will discuss the importance of healthy eating for mental health, provide examples of nutrient-rich foods, and offer tips for maintaining a healthy diet.

Sleep

Getting adequate and restful sleep is essential for mental health. Lack of sleep can contribute to irritability, mood swings, and poor cognitive functioning. In contrast, good sleep hygiene can lead to improved mood, memory, and concentration. In this section, we will explore the importance of sleep for mental health, provide tips for improving sleep hygiene, and discuss common sleep disorders.

❖ Mindfulness and Relaxation Techniques

In addition to physical self-care, mental self-care is equally important for overall well-being. Mindfulness and relaxation techniques can help reduce stress, promote relaxation, and improve mood. Examples of such techniques include meditation, deep breathing exercises, and progressive muscle relaxation. In this section, we will discuss the benefits of mindfulness and relaxation techniques, and offer tips for incorporating them into daily life.

- ❖ Creative Outlets

Engaging in creative activities, such as painting, writing, or playing music, can be a valuable form of self-care. These activities can provide a sense of purpose, increase self-esteem, and promote relaxation. In this section, we will explore the benefits of creative outlets for mental health, provide examples of creative activities, and offer tips for incorporating them into daily life.

Conclusion: Prioritizing Self-care for Improved Mental Health

In summary, self-care techniques such as exercise, healthy eating, sleep, mindfulness and relaxation techniques, and creative outlets can all contribute to improved mental health after a life-changing event. It is important to prioritize self-care as a part of one's daily routine, and to find techniques that work best for individual needs and preferences. By prioritizing self-care, individuals can take important steps towards improving their mental health and overall well-being.

Mindfulness and Relaxation Techniques

In today's fast-paced and constantly connected world, it can be challenging to take a step back and just be present in the moment. The stress and anxiety of daily life can take a toll on our mental and physical health, leading to a range of issues such as insomnia, depression, and burnout. That's where mindfulness and relaxation techniques come in - these practices can help us cultivate a sense of calm, reduce stress, and improve our overall well-being.

In this chapter, we'll explore the benefits of mindfulness and relaxation techniques and provide examples of exercises you can try to incorporate these practices into your daily life.

I. What are Mindfulness and Relaxation Techniques?

Mindfulness is the practice of being present in the moment and observing one's thoughts and feelings without judgment. It involves intentionally focusing on the present moment and acknowledging and accepting one's experiences without getting caught up in them.

Relaxation techniques are activities that help reduce stress and promote relaxation in the body and mind. These can include deep breathing exercises, progressive muscle relaxation, and visualization.

II. Benefits of Mindfulness and Relaxation Techniques

Reduced Stress and Anxiety: Mindfulness and relaxation techniques have been shown to reduce symptoms of stress and anxiety by activating the body's relaxation response.

Improved Sleep: These practices can also improve sleep quality by helping to quiet the mind and relax the body before bedtime.

Enhanced Mental Health: Mindfulness and relaxation techniques can improve overall mental health by reducing symptoms of depression and promoting positive emotions.

Better Physical Health: Studies have found that these practices can lower blood pressure, reduce chronic pain, and improve the immune system's function.

Mindfulness and Relaxation Techniques to Try

Mindful Breathing: Focus on your breath and observe its natural rhythm. Notice the sensation of the air moving in and out of your body.

Body Scan Meditation: Start at the top of your head and work your way down, paying attention to each part of your body and any sensations you feel.

Progressive Muscle Relaxation: Tense and then relax different muscle groups throughout the body, focusing on the feeling of relaxation as the tension releases.

Different Hertz frequencies have been associated with different benefits, although scientific research is still limited in this area. Here are some commonly suggested frequencies for meditation and their associated benefits:

432 Hz: Believed to be a natural frequency that is in harmony with nature and can promote healing and well-being.
528 Hz: Also known as the "Love Frequency," believed to promote a sense of peace, love, and well-being.
639 Hz: Believed to promote harmony and balance in relationships, as well as enhance communication and understanding.
741 Hz: Believed to promote the removal of toxins and negativity from the body, as well as promote creativity and problem-solving.
852 Hz: Believed to promote spiritual awakening and enlightenment.

It's important to note that while some people may find these frequencies helpful in their meditation practice, there is limited scientific research to support their specific benefits. Additionally, it's always a good idea to consult with a healthcare professional if you are experiencing depression or other mental health concerns.

Visualization: Imagine a peaceful scene, such as a beach or forest, and focus on the details of the environment.

Yoga: A practice that combines physical movement with mindfulness and relaxation techniques.

IV. Incorporating Mindfulness and Relaxation into Daily Life

Set aside time each day for mindfulness or relaxation practices.

Find a quiet space where you can focus without distractions.

Experiment with different techniques to find what works best for you.

Incorporate mindfulness into everyday activities, such as walking or eating.

Practice self-compassion and be patient with yourself as you learn to cultivate mindfulness and relaxation.

Conclusion

Incorporating mindfulness and relaxation techniques into your daily routine can have a significant impact on your mental and physical health. By taking time to focus on the present moment and quiet your mind, you can reduce stress, improve sleep, and enhance overall well-being. With a little practice and patience, anyone can learn to incorporate these practices into their daily life and reap the benefits.

Creative Outlets

Life-changing events can cause emotional turmoil and stress, leaving us feeling lost and uncertain about the future. During these challenging times, creative outlets can be a valuable tool for coping and healing. Whether it's painting, writing, music, or other forms of art, creative expression can help us process our emotions, gain new perspectives, and find a sense of peace and joy in our lives.

In this section, we will explore the benefits of creative outlets for mental health, the science behind it, and various examples of creative activities that you can incorporate into your life. We will also provide practical exercises and tips to help you get started and stay motivated.

Benefits of Creative Outlets for Mental Health:

Engaging in creative activities can have numerous benefits for our mental health, including:

Stress relief: Art can be a form of relaxation and stress relief. By focusing on the creative process, we can forget about our worries and feel a sense of calm.

Emotional expression: Art can provide a healthy outlet for expressing our emotions, including difficult or painful ones that we may not feel comfortable sharing verbally.

Self-discovery: Creative activities can help us explore and discover new aspects of ourselves, our interests, and our passions.

Increased self-esteem: Completing a creative project can boost our confidence and self-esteem, providing a sense of accomplishment and pride.

Improved cognitive function: Studies have shown that creative activities can enhance cognitive function, including memory, problem-solving, and decision-making.

Science behind the Benefits:
The benefits of creative activities on mental health can be attributed to their impact on our brain's neuroplasticity. Neuroplasticity refers to the brain's ability to reorganize itself by forming new neural connections throughout life. When we engage in creative activities, we stimulate the brain's reward system, releasing dopamine and promoting the growth of new neural connections. This process can improve mood, decrease anxiety, and enhance cognitive function.

Examples of Creative Outlets:

There are countless creative activities to choose from, including:

- Painting, drawing, and coloring
- Writing, journaling, and storytelling
- Playing music, singing, and dancing
- Photography and videography
- Crafting and DIY projects
- Cooking and baking
- Gardening and landscaping
- Acting and performing
- Learning a new language or instrument
- Graphic design and digital art

Exercises and Tips to Get Started:

Here are some exercises and tips to help you get started with your creative outlet:

Set aside time for your creative activity: Schedule time in your day or week to engage in your chosen activity, and make it a priority.

Gather materials: Make sure you have all the necessary materials for your chosen activity. Consider investing in high-quality materials if it's a hobby you plan to continue.

Take a class or workshop: Consider taking a class or workshop to learn new techniques and connect with other like-minded individuals.

Start small: Don't overwhelm yourself with a complicated project. Start with small, manageable tasks and work your way up.

Experiment: Don't be afraid to experiment and try new things. You may discover a new passion or interest.

Embrace imperfection: Remember that the creative process is about the journey, not the destination. Embrace imperfection and allow yourself to make mistakes.

Conclusion:

Creative outlets can be a powerful tool for coping with life-changing events and promoting mental health. By engaging in a creative activity, we can express ourselves, reduce stress, and discover new aspects of ourselves. Whether it's painting, writing, music, or other forms of art, there are countless options to choose from. By incorporating creative activities into our daily lives, we can find a sense of joy and fulfillment that can help us cope with difficult emotions and experiences.

In conclusion, it's important to remember that coping with life-changing events can be a challenging and ongoing process. It's okay to seek help and support from friends, family, and mental health professionals. In addition, incorporating self-care techniques, mindfulness and relaxation techniques, and creative outlets into our daily routines can provide additional support and coping mechanisms.

It's important to find what works best for us as individuals and to prioritize our mental health and well-being. By taking care of ourselves, we can better navigate the ups and downs of life and find a sense of resilience and strength within ourselves. Remember that we are all capable of healing and growing from life-changing events, and that we are never alone in our journeys.

Mindfulness practices and meditation exercises

Journal Exercises:

Take 10 minutes to write about your daily experiences with mindfulness and meditation. What techniques have you found helpful?

_____
_____
_____
_____
_____
_____
_____
_____
_____
_____
_____
_____
_____
_____

What challenges have you encountered?

_____
_____

How have these practices impacted your overall well-being?

Write a letter to your future self about your goals for incorporating mindfulness and meditation into your daily life. What benefits do you hope to gain from these practices?

How will you stay motivated to continue?

___

Reflect on a recent experience where you felt overwhelmed or stressed. Write about how you could have applied mindfulness and meditation techniques in that moment to help manage your emotions.

___

Quiz Questions:

What is the purpose of mindfulness practices and meditation?

How can mindfulness and meditation benefit our mental and physical health?

What are some common techniques used in mindfulness and meditation practices?

How often should someone practice mindfulness and meditation to see benefits?

What is the difference between mindfulness and meditation?

Survey Questions:

How often do you practice mindfulness and meditation?
What techniques do you find most helpful in your mindfulness and meditation practices?

Have you noticed any changes in your mental or physical health since incorporating mindfulness and meditation into your daily routine?
What challenges have you encountered while practicing mindfulness and meditation?
What motivates you to continue practicing mindfulness and meditation?

Essay Topic:
Reflect on the benefits of mindfulness practices and meditation for mental health. Discuss the science behind these practices and their potential impact on the brain and overall well-being. Provide examples of successful implementation of these practices in real-world situations and discuss how they can be incorporated into daily life to promote mental wellness.

Connecting with supportive friends and family members

When life gets tough, having a supportive network of friends and family members can make all the difference. Not only can they provide emotional support, but they can also offer practical help and guidance. In this chapter, we will explore the benefits of connecting with supportive friends and family members, and how to foster those relationships for greater mental and emotional well-being.

The Importance of Supportive Relationships:

Humans are social creatures, and the connections we have with others play a critical role in our overall health and happiness. Research has shown that having strong social support can reduce the negative effects of stress, improve our immune system, and increase our resilience in the face of difficult life events.

Having supportive friends and family members can provide a range of benefits, including:

Emotional support: Talking to someone who understands what you are going through and can offer a listening ear can be incredibly healing and validating.

Practical support: Friends and family can help with daily tasks such as cooking, cleaning, or running errands, which can be especially helpful during times of stress or illness.

Advice and guidance: Sometimes, we need a fresh perspective or someone to bounce ideas off of. Having a supportive friend or family member can provide valuable insights and advice.

Fun and enjoyment: Spending time with people we enjoy and who make us laugh can be an effective way to relieve stress and boost our mood.

Building Supportive Relationships:

While having supportive friends and family members is important, it's not always easy to cultivate those relationships. Here are some tips for building and maintaining strong connections:

Be intentional: Make an effort to reach out to people and schedule regular check-ins or get-togethers. Even small gestures such as sending a text or card can go a long way.
Show appreciation: Let the people in your life know how much you value their support and friendship. Express gratitude for the things they do and the qualities you admire in them.

Be vulnerable: Sharing your own struggles and vulnerabilities can help build trust and deepen connections with others.

Listen actively: When someone is sharing their own struggles, be sure to listen without judgment and offer empathy and support.

Be reliable: Follow through on commitments and be there for the people in your life when they need you.

Connecting Virtually:

In today's world, connecting with supportive friends and family members doesn't always mean meeting in person. Virtual communication platforms such as video calls, phone calls, and messaging apps can be just as effective in maintaining strong relationships. Additionally, online support groups or forums can provide a sense of community and understanding for those who may not have a strong network of support in their immediate vicinity.

Exercise 1: Journal Prompt

Think about the people in your life who are the most supportive and uplifting. Reflect on what qualities you admire in them, and how they make you feel when you are with them. Consider ways in which you can deepen those relationships or show your appreciation for them.

_____
_____
_____
_____
_____
_____
_____
_____
_____
_____
_____
_____
_____

Quiz

How can having supportive friends and family members benefit our mental and emotional well-being?
a. Provide emotional support
b. Offer practical help and guidance
c. Both a and b
d. None of the above

What is one way to build and maintain strong connections with others?
a. Be vulnerable
b. Listen actively
c. Show appreciation
d. All of the above

Can virtual communication platforms be effective in maintaining strong relationships?
a. Yes
b. No

Exercise 3: Survey

Take a moment to reach out to the people in your life who you consider to be the most supportive and uplifting. Ask them how you can be a better friend or family member to them, and what they appreciate most about your relationship. Use their responses to guide your efforts in strengthening those connections.

Exercise 4: Practice Active Listening

One of the most important ways to connect with others is through active listening. When we actively listen, we are fully present in the moment and focused on what the other person is saying. This means not only hearing the words they are saying, but also paying attention to their tone of voice, body language, and emotions.

To practice active listening, try the following exercise:

Choose a friend or family member to have a conversation with.
Before the conversation, take a few deep breaths and clear your mind of any distractions.
During the conversation, focus on the other person and give them your full attention.
Resist the urge to interrupt or interject your own thoughts or opinions. Instead, ask open-ended questions to encourage them to share more about their thoughts and feelings.
Paraphrase what they have said to show that you have understood and are actively listening.
Validate their emotions and feelings by acknowledging them and showing empathy.
End the conversation with a gesture of appreciation, such as a hug or a kind word.
By practicing active listening, you can deepen your connections with others and strengthen your relationships.

Exercise 5: Write a Gratitude Letter

Expressing gratitude can help us feel more connected to others and improve our overall well-being. One way to practice gratitude is by writing a gratitude letter to someone in your life who has made a positive impact on you.

To write a gratitude letter, follow these steps:

Choose someone who has had a significant impact on your life in a positive way.
Write a letter to that person expressing your gratitude and appreciation for what they have done for you.
Be specific about how they have helped you and what you admire about them.
Take the time to really think about what you want to say and how you want to express your gratitude.
When you're finished, consider reading the letter to the person in person or over the phone.
By expressing gratitude, we can strengthen our relationships and deepen our connections with others.

_____
_____
_____
_____
_____
_____
_____
_____
_____
_____
_____
_____
_____
_____
_____
_____
_____
_____
_____
_____

Conclusion

Connecting with supportive friends and family members is essential for our overall well-being. By taking the time to cultivate and strengthen these relationships, we can improve our mental and emotional health, reduce stress, and increase our happiness and sense of belonging. Whether it's through simple acts of kindness, active listening, or expressing gratitude, there are countless ways to connect with others and build strong, supportive relationships. So reach out to your loved ones, show them how much you appreciate them, and enjoy the many benefits that come with strong social connections.

Joining support groups or seeking professional counseling

At some point in our lives, we may find ourselves struggling with various challenges, such as mental health issues, relationship problems, or grief. During such times, seeking support from others can be crucial to our well-being. Joining support groups or seeking professional counseling are two ways to access this support. In this chapter, we will explore the benefits of these options, how they work, and how to access them.

Benefits of joining support groups

Joining a support group can have many benefits, including:

A sense of community: Support groups provide a sense of community and connection with others who are experiencing similar challenges. This can be especially important during times when we feel isolated or alone.

Validation and understanding: Being in a support group can provide validation and understanding of our experiences, which can be therapeutic in itself. We may find comfort in hearing from others who have gone through similar challenges and have come out on the other side.

Coping strategies: Support groups can provide us with coping strategies and tools to manage our challenges. Members may share their own experiences and offer practical advice for dealing with difficult situations.

Increased self-esteem: Being a member of a support group can increase our sense of self-worth and self-esteem. We may feel empowered by sharing our own experiences and offering support to others.

Improved mental health: Research has shown that participating in support groups can lead to improved mental health outcomes, including decreased symptoms of depression and anxiety.

How support groups work

Support groups can take many forms, from in-person meetings to online forums. Some are facilitated by professionals, such as therapists or social workers, while others are peer-led. Regardless of the format, support groups typically involve:

Sharing experiences: Members share their own experiences with the group, including their challenges, successes, and setbacks.

Active listening: Members listen actively and provide support and validation to others in the group.

Confidentiality: Members agree to keep what is shared within the group confidential, creating a safe and trusting environment.

Supportive feedback: Members offer feedback and support to each other, which can include practical advice, encouragement, and empathy.

There are many ways to access support groups, including:

Online: Many support groups are available online, either through social media platforms or specialized websites.

Local organizations: Local organizations, such as community centers, churches, or hospitals, may offer support groups for specific issues or populations.

National organizations: National organizations, such as the National Alliance on Mental Illness (NAMI) or the American Cancer Society, offer support groups for a range of challenges.

Professional referrals: Mental health professionals, such as therapists or psychiatrists, may be able to refer you to a support group that is appropriate for your needs.

Benefits of seeking professional counseling

Seeking professional counseling can also have many benefits, including:

Expert guidance: Professional counselors are trained to help individuals navigate difficult challenges and can provide expert guidance and support.

A safe space to explore emotions: Counseling sessions provide a safe space to explore our emotions and thoughts, which can be difficult to do with friends or family members.

Personalized treatment: Counselors can develop personalized treatment plans that are tailored to our specific needs and goals.

Improved relationships: Counseling can help us improve our relationships with others by providing us with tools and strategies for effective communication and conflict resolution.

Improved mental health: Research has shown that counseling can lead to improved mental health outcomes, including decreased symptoms of anxiety and depression.

How counseling works

Counseling typically involves:

Assessment: During the first session, the counselor will ask questions to assess your current situation, your goals for counseling, and any past experiences or trauma that may be contributing to your current struggles. They will also discuss their approach to counseling and what you can expect from the sessions.

Individualized Treatment Plan: Based on the assessment, the counselor will create an individualized treatment plan that outlines the goals of counseling and the methods that will be used to achieve those goals. This plan will be reviewed and updated as needed throughout the counseling process.

Therapeutic Techniques: A variety of therapeutic techniques may be used in counseling, including cognitive-behavioral therapy (CBT), mindfulness-based therapy, and psychodynamic therapy. The counselor will work with you to determine which techniques will be most effective for your unique situation.

Regular Sessions: Counseling typically involves regular sessions that are scheduled in advance. The frequency of sessions may vary depending on your needs and the counselor's approach to treatment.

Progress Monitoring: Throughout the counseling process, the counselor will monitor your progress and adjust the treatment plan as needed. They may also ask you to complete self-assessments or other measures to track your progress.

Benefits of Counseling

Joining a support group or seeking professional counseling can provide numerous benefits for mental health and overall well-being. Some of the benefits of counseling include:

Improved Coping Skills: Counseling can help you develop effective coping skills for dealing with stress, anxiety, and other challenges.

Increased Self-Awareness: Through counseling, you can gain a better understanding of your thoughts, feelings, and behaviors, and learn how to change them for the better.

Improved Relationships: Counseling can also help you improve your relationships with others by teaching you effective communication skills and helping you work through conflicts.

Reduced Symptoms: For those struggling with mental health issues, counseling can help reduce symptoms such as anxiety, depression, and PTSD.

Increased Resilience: By building coping skills and improving self-awareness, counseling can help you become more resilient and better equipped to handle future challenges.

Success Stories

There are countless success stories of people who have benefited from joining support groups or seeking professional counseling. Here are a few examples:

Sarah was struggling with anxiety and depression after a traumatic event in her life. She started attending a support group for survivors of trauma and found immense comfort in connecting with others who had been through similar experiences. With the support of the group, Sarah was able to work through her trauma and develop coping skills for managing her anxiety and depression.

John had been struggling with substance abuse for years and had tried numerous times to quit on his own without success. He finally decided to seek professional counseling and started working with a therapist who specialized in addiction. Through counseling, John was able to identify the root causes of his addiction and develop a plan for recovery. With the support of his therapist and a 12-step program, John has been sober for over a year.

Amanda had always struggled with self-esteem and confidence issues. She started seeing a counselor who specialized in cognitive-behavioral therapy and learned techniques for challenging her negative thoughts and building self-confidence. With the help of her counselor, Amanda was able to overcome her self-esteem issues and start living a more fulfilling life.

Conclusion

Joining support groups or seeking professional counseling can be a powerful tool for improving mental health and overall well-being. By connecting with others who have shared experiences or seeking the guidance of a trained professional, individuals can gain the support, coping skills, and self-awareness they need to overcome challenges and achieve their goals. If you or someone you know is struggling with mental health issues, consider reaching out to a support group or counselor to explore your options for support and healing. Remember, seeking help is a sign of strength, and it is never too late to start on the path to recovery and growth.

Moving Forward: Thriving after a Life-Changing Event

Life is full of unexpected twists and turns, and sometimes we find ourselves facing major challenges that completely alter the course of our lives. Whether it's a serious illness, a traumatic experience, or a significant loss, these events can leave us feeling overwhelmed, lost, and unsure of how to move forward. But as difficult as these situations may be, they also present an opportunity for growth, resilience, and transformation. In this chapter, we will explore strategies for thriving after a life-changing event, from cultivating a growth mindset to building a strong support system. With these tools in hand, you can not only overcome the challenges you face but also emerge from them stronger and more resilient than ever before.

Developing resilience and bouncing back after adversity

Life is full of unexpected events, some of which can have a profound impact on our physical, mental, and emotional well-being. Whether it's the loss of a loved one, a health crisis, a job loss, or any other major life change, it's normal to feel overwhelmed, anxious, and uncertain about what the future holds. However, it's important to remember that adversity can also bring growth and opportunities for personal development.

Developing resilience is essential for bouncing back after adversity and thriving in the face of challenges. Resilience is the ability to adapt and recover from difficult situations, to keep going even when things seem impossible. It's not about being invincible or never experiencing stress, but rather about having the skills and mindset to cope with stress and overcome obstacles.

In this chapter, we will explore the concept of resilience and the factors that contribute to it. We will discuss practical strategies for building resilience, including mindset shifts, coping skills, and social support. We will also examine the latest research on resilience and highlight inspiring success stories of individuals who have overcome adversity and emerged stronger than ever.

So if you're looking to develop resilience and bounce back after a life-changing event, you've come to the right place. Let's get started.

Understanding Resilience

Resilience is a complex concept that involves a combination of internal and external factors. In this section, we'll take a closer look at what resilience is and what factors contribute to it.

What is Resilience?

Resilience is the ability to adapt and recover from difficult or challenging situations. It's not about avoiding stress or never experiencing adversity, but rather about being able to bounce back and thrive despite it. Resilience is not a fixed trait, but rather a set of skills and behaviors that can be developed and strengthened over time.

Factors That Contribute to Resilience

While resilience is a multifaceted concept, there are several factors that have been shown to contribute to resilience. These include:

- Positive self-talk and mindset
- Social support and connectedness
- Coping skills and problem-solving abilities
- Optimism and hope
- Flexibility and adaptability
- Sense of purpose and meaning

Section 2: Building Resilience

Now that we have a better understanding of what resilience is and what factors contribute to it, let's explore practical strategies for building resilience.

Mindset Shifts

One of the most important factors in building resilience is having a positive mindset. This doesn't mean ignoring or denying difficult emotions or situations, but rather reframing them in a more positive light. Some helpful mindset shifts for building resilience include:

Reframing challenges as opportunities for growth
Focusing on what you can control rather than what you can't
Practicing gratitude and focusing on what you have rather than what you lack

Coping Skills

Developing effective coping skills is essential for building resilience. Coping skills are strategies for managing stress and difficult emotions, and they can include:

- Deep breathing and relaxation techniques

- Mindfulness meditation

- Exercise and physical activity

- Creative outlets, such as art or music

- Social Support

Having a strong support system is a key factor in building resilience. Social support can come from family, friends, coworkers, or support groups, and it can include:

- Emotional support, such as empathy and validation

- Practical support, such as help with daily tasks or financial assistance

- Informational support, such as advice and guidance

- Optimism and Hope

Optimism and hope are powerful tools for building resilience. Cultivating a sense of optimism and hope can help you see the potential for positive outcomes even in the face of adversity. Some strategies to develop optimism and hope include:

Practicing Gratitude: Gratitude is the act of being thankful for the good things in life. When we focus on what we have, rather than what we don't have, it can shift our perspective and help us to see the positive aspects of our lives. A daily gratitude practice can be as simple as writing down three things you're grateful for each day.

Reframing: Reframing is the process of looking at a situation in a new way. It involves shifting your perspective from a negative outlook to a more positive one. For example, instead of seeing a setback as a failure, you could reframe it as a learning opportunity.

Positive self-talk: The way we talk to ourselves can have a big impact on our outlook and resilience. Practicing positive self-talk can help us to challenge negative beliefs and replace them with more positive ones. For example, instead of thinking "I'm not good enough," you could reframe it as "I'm doing the best I can, and that's enough."

Visualization: Visualization is a technique that involves imagining positive outcomes. It can help to build confidence and motivation, as well as reduce anxiety and stress. To practice visualization, find a quiet place where you won't be disturbed and imagine yourself achieving your goals or overcoming challenges.

Connect with Others: Building strong relationships with friends, family, or a community can help to boost resilience. Having supportive people in your life can provide emotional support, practical help, and a sense of belonging. Social connection can also help to reduce stress and improve mental health.

Practice Self-Care: Taking care of yourself physically, emotionally, and mentally is essential for building resilience. This can include getting enough sleep, eating a balanced diet, exercising regularly, and engaging in activities that bring you joy.

Acceptance: Accepting that life is unpredictable and that adversity is a part of life can help to build resilience. Rather than trying to control every aspect of your life, focus on what you can control and let go of what you can't.

In summary, developing resilience is essential for bouncing back after adversity. Strategies such as practicing gratitude, reframing negative beliefs, positive self-talk, visualization, connecting with others, practicing self-care, and acceptance can help to cultivate resilience and build a more positive outlook on life. Remember, resilience is not something you're born with - it's a skill that can be developed and strengthened over time. By focusing on these strategies and building a support system, you can thrive even in the face of adversity.

Setting realistic goals and taking small steps towards achieving them

Setting goals can be a powerful tool for personal growth and development. Whether you're looking to improve your physical health, advance your career, or build stronger relationships, having clear and achievable goals can help you stay focused and motivated. However, setting unrealistic goals or trying to tackle too much at once can lead to frustration, disappointment, and burnout. In this chapter, we will explore the importance of setting realistic goals and taking small steps towards achieving them. We will also discuss some practical strategies for setting and reaching your goals, and share some inspiring success stories of people who have achieved their goals through determination and perseverance.

Why Setting Realistic Goals is Important:

Setting realistic goals is important for several reasons:

Increases motivation and focus: Setting clear, achievable goals can help you stay motivated and focused on your priorities. When you have a specific goal in mind, you're more likely to take action towards achieving it.

Reduces stress and anxiety: Unrealistic goals can create unnecessary stress and anxiety. When you set goals that are too difficult or unrealistic, you're setting yourself up for failure and disappointment.

Improves self-confidence: Achieving small goals can boost your self-confidence and help you feel more capable of tackling larger challenges.

Increases accountability: When you set clear goals and share them with others, you're more likely to follow through on your commitments and stay accountable.

Strategies for Setting and Achieving Realistic Goals:

Start with a vision: Before setting specific goals, it's important to have a clear vision of what you want to achieve. Take some time to reflect on your values, passions, and priorities, and think about what you want your life to look like in the future.

Make your goals specific and measurable: Instead of setting vague goals like "get in shape" or "be more productive," try to make your goals specific and measurable. For example, "exercise for 30 minutes a day, 3 times a week" or "complete one important task each day."

Break your goals into smaller steps: Instead of trying to tackle your goals all at once, break them into smaller, more manageable steps. This will help you stay motivated and focused, and make your goals feel more achievable.

Track your progress: Keep track of your progress towards your goals, and celebrate your successes along the way. This can help you stay motivated and focused, and give you a sense of accomplishment.

Be flexible and adapt: Life is unpredictable, and sometimes things don't go as planned. Be flexible and willing to adapt your goals as needed, and don't be too hard on yourself if you need to change your course of action.

Success Stories:

Bill had always dreamed of running a marathon, but had never been a runner. Instead of signing up for a marathon right away, he set a goal to run for 10 minutes a day, 3 times a week. He gradually increased his running time and distance, and after several months of training, he successfully completed his first marathon.

Emily had a busy job and a young family, and struggled to find time for herself. She set a goal to wake up 30 minutes earlier each day, and use that time for yoga and meditation. She gradually built up her practice, and found that the extra time for self-care helped her feel more centered and focused throughout the day.

Tom had always been interested in learning a new language, but didn't have the time or resources to take formal classes. He set a goal to practice for 10 minutes a day using an online language learning program. Over time, he built up his skills and confidence, and eventually was able to have basic conversations in his target language.

Conclusion:

Setting realistic goals and taking small steps towards achieving them is a powerful strategy for developing resilience and achieving success in all areas of life. By breaking down larger goals into smaller, manageable tasks, you can build momentum, increase your sense of accomplishment, and stay motivated even when faced with obstacles.

Remember to keep your goals SMART (specific, measurable, achievable, relevant, and time-bound) and to celebrate your progress along the way. Celebrating small wins can help you stay positive and energized, and can make the journey towards your larger goals more enjoyable.

Don't be afraid to seek support from others when setting and working towards your goals. Having a supportive network can provide encouragement, accountability, and guidance when you need it most.

Finally, be kind to yourself. Remember that setbacks and obstacles are a normal part of the journey towards achieving any goal. By practicing self-compassion and focusing on progress rather than perfection, you can develop the resilience and perseverance needed to overcome challenges and achieve your dreams.

So take a deep breath, reflect on your values and priorities, and start setting goals that are meaningful and achievable for you. Remember that every small step counts, and that with patience, persistence, and a positive mindset, you can accomplish anything you set your mind to.

Finding purpose and meaning in life after a traumatic event

Traumatic events can upend our sense of purpose and meaning in life. They can shake our core beliefs and values, leaving us feeling lost and unsure of our direction. However, finding purpose and meaning after a traumatic event can be a powerful tool for building resilience and moving forward. In this chapter, we will explore the importance of finding purpose and meaning after trauma, provide examples of individuals who have done so, and offer practical exercises and tools to help you identify your own sense of purpose and meaning.

The Importance of Finding Purpose and Meaning:

Finding purpose and meaning after a traumatic event can be a critical step in the healing process. It can help us make sense of what has happened to us and provide us with a sense of control over our lives.

Purpose and meaning can also help us build resilience, providing us with the motivation to keep moving forward and the ability to bounce back from setbacks.

Examples of Finding Purpose and Meaning:

There are countless examples of individuals who have found purpose and meaning in the aftermath of trauma. One example is Malala Yousafzai, who was shot by the Taliban in Pakistan for advocating for girls' education. After her recovery, Malala became a global advocate for education and women's rights, ultimately winning the Nobel Peace Prize at just 17 years old.

Another example is Elizabeth Smart, who was kidnapped at the age of 14 and held captive for nine months. After her rescue, Elizabeth became an advocate for victims of abuse and has dedicated her life to helping others find their voice and heal from trauma.

Journal Exercises:

Journaling can be a powerful tool for exploring and identifying our sense of purpose and meaning. The following exercises can help you get started:

Write a letter to your future self. Imagine that you are writing to yourself in five years. What do you want your life to look like? What goals do you hope to have achieved?

_____
_____
_____
_____
_____

What values are most important to you?

Write about a time when you felt the most fulfilled in life. What were you doing?

What made that experience so meaningful to you?

Reflect on a challenge or adversity you have faced. How did you grow or learn from that experience?

Did it change your perspective on life or your goals for the future?

Question Quiz:

Why is finding purpose and meaning important after a traumatic event?
a. It can help us make sense of what has happened to us
b. It can provide us with a sense of control over our lives
c. It can help us build resilience
d. All of the above

Who is an example of someone who found purpose and meaning after trauma?
a. Malala Yousafzai
b. Elizabeth Smart
c. Both a and b
d. Neither a nor b

What is one journal exercise for exploring your sense of purpose and meaning?
a. Write a letter to your past self
b. Write about a time when you felt the most bored in life
c. Reflect on a time when you were not successful in achieving your goals
d. Write a letter to your future self

What is resilience?
a. The ability to bounce back from setbacks
b. The ability to avoid adversity altogether
c. The ability to ignore negative thoughts and emotions
d. None of the above

How can purpose and meaning help build resilience?
a. By providing us with motivation to keep moving forward
b. By giving us a sense of control over our lives
c. By helping us make sense of what has happened to us
d. Both a and b

What is a potential benefit of finding purpose and meaning after trauma?

a. Improved mental health and well-being
b. Increased job satisfaction
c. Improved relationships with others
d. All of the above

Finding purpose and meaning after a traumatic event can lead to many positive outcomes, including improved mental health and well-being, increased job satisfaction, and improved relationships with others. When we have a sense of purpose, we feel that our lives have meaning and that our actions are making a difference. This can help us feel more fulfilled and satisfied with our lives.

One study found that people who had experienced trauma and had found a sense of purpose and meaning in their lives reported higher levels of psychological well-being and life satisfaction compared to those who had not found purpose and meaning (Steger, Kashdan, Sullivan, & Lorentz, 2008).

Journal Exercises
Journaling can be a helpful tool for exploring our thoughts and feelings and gaining clarity about our values and priorities. Here are a few journaling exercises that can help with finding purpose and meaning after trauma:

1. Reflect on your values
Think about what is most important to you in life. What values do you hold dear? What principles guide your decision-making? Write down your answers and reflect on how you can incorporate these values into your daily life.

_____
_____
_____
_____
_____

2. Explore your passions
Think about what you love to do. What brings you joy and fulfillment? Write down your answers and reflect on how you can incorporate these passions into your life more often.

3. Set goals
Think about what you want to achieve in the short-term and long-term. Write down your goals and reflect on how they align with your values and passions. Consider breaking down larger goals into smaller, more manageable steps to make them feel less daunting.

Question Quiz

True or False: Finding purpose and meaning after trauma is not important for mental health and well-being.

True or False: Having a sense of purpose can lead to increased job satisfaction.

What is one potential benefit of finding purpose and meaning after trauma?

What is one way to explore your values?

What is one way to explore your passions?

Why might it be helpful to break down larger goals into smaller, more manageable steps?

True or False: You can only find purpose and meaning in work-related activities.

True or False: Finding purpose and meaning after trauma is a one-time event.

What is one potential outcome of journaling?

True or False: Everyone has the same values and passions.

Personal survey

Please answer the following questions to help us better understand your experiences with finding purpose and meaning after trauma:

Have you experienced trauma?

Yes
No

Have you found purpose and meaning in your life after trauma?

Yes
No
Not sure

If you answered yes to question 2, how did you find purpose and meaning? (check all that apply)

Through work or career-related activities
Through hobbies or leisure activities
Through relationships with others
Through spiritual or religious practices
Other (please specify)

If you answered no to question 2, what barriers have you encountered in finding purpose and meaning? (check all that apply)

Lack of motivation
Feeling overwhelmed
Not sure where to start
Difficulty identifying values and priorities
Other (please specify)

On a scale of 1-10, how important is finding purpose and meaning in your life after trauma?

1 (not important)
10 (very important)

Celebrating progress and recognizing accomplishments

Making progress towards our goals can be a challenging journey. It can be easy to get caught up in the day-to-day struggles and lose sight of how far we've come. However, it's essential to celebrate progress and recognize accomplishments along the way. Celebrating progress can help motivate us to keep going and remind us that our hard work is paying off. In this chapter, we will explore the importance of celebrating progress and recognizing accomplishments, strategies for celebrating progress, and the benefits of doing so.

Why is celebrating progress and recognizing accomplishments important?

Celebrating progress and recognizing accomplishments are essential for several reasons:

Increases motivation: Celebrating progress and recognizing accomplishments can help increase motivation. It helps us feel a sense of pride in our achievements and reminds us of the progress we've made.

Builds confidence: Recognizing our accomplishments can help build our confidence. It's important to acknowledge and celebrate our successes, no matter how small they may seem.

Fosters a positive mindset: Celebrating progress helps foster a positive mindset. It helps us focus on the positive aspects of our journey and reminds us that our hard work is paying off.

Encourages perseverance: Recognizing our accomplishments helps encourage perseverance. It reminds us that our hard work and dedication are worth it and encourages us to keep going.

Strategies for celebrating progress

Keep a progress journal: Keeping a progress journal is an excellent way to track your progress and reflect on your accomplishments. Write down your successes, no matter how small, and take the time to reflect on how far you've come.

Share your progress with others: Sharing your progress with others can be a great way to celebrate your accomplishments. It can be helpful to have a support system that can cheer you on and remind you of your progress.

Take a break: Taking a break is an essential part of celebrating progress. Sometimes, we need to take a step back and reflect on our journey. Take some time to relax and recharge, and celebrate your hard work.

Reward yourself: Rewards can be a great way to celebrate your accomplishments. Treat yourself to something you've been wanting, like a massage or a fancy dinner.

Create a vision board: Creating a vision board can be a great way to celebrate progress and visualize your future goals. Use pictures and quotes that inspire you and remind you of your progress.

Benefits of celebrating progress and recognizing accomplishments

Increased motivation: Celebrating progress and recognizing accomplishments can help increase motivation. It helps us feel a sense of pride in our achievements and reminds us of the progress we've made.

Boosts confidence: Recognizing our accomplishments can help build our confidence. It's important to acknowledge and celebrate our successes, no matter how small they may seem.

Fosters a positive mindset: Celebrating progress helps foster a positive mindset. It helps us focus on the positive aspects of our journey and reminds us that our hard work is paying off.

Encourages perseverance: Recognizing our accomplishments helps encourage perseverance. It reminds us that our hard work and dedication are worth it and encourages us to keep going.

Reduces stress: Celebrating progress can also help reduce stress. It can be easy to get caught up in the day-to-day struggles of our journey, and celebrating progress can help us relax and reflect on our hard work.

Examples of celebrating progress

Running a marathon: Running a marathon is an excellent example of celebrating progress. It takes months of training and dedication to complete a marathon, and crossing the finish line is a significant accomplishment.

Graduating from college: Graduating from college is a significant accomplishment that deserves to be celebrated. It takes years of hard work and dedication to earn a degree, and graduation day is a time to reflect on the journey and feel proud of the achievement. It's a milestone moment that signifies the end of one chapter and the beginning of another. However, celebrating progress and recognizing accomplishments is not just limited to major milestones like graduating from college. It's something that we should do regularly in our lives to maintain a positive mindset and motivate ourselves to keep moving forward. In this chapter, we'll explore the importance of celebrating progress and recognizing accomplishments, and provide tips on how to do so effectively.

Why is celebrating progress and recognizing accomplishments important?

Boosts self-esteem and confidence: Celebrating progress and recognizing accomplishments can boost our self-esteem and confidence. It helps us to acknowledge our hard work and dedication, and feel proud of our achievements. This positive self-talk can help to build self-confidence and motivate us to continue striving towards our goals.

Provides motivation: Celebrating progress and recognizing accomplishments provides us with motivation to continue working towards our goals. By acknowledging and celebrating our progress, we are reminded of our abilities and strengths, which can give us the boost we need to keep moving forward.

Encourages gratitude: Recognizing our accomplishments encourages us to be grateful for what we have achieved, and for the people who have helped us along the way. This gratitude can lead to positive emotions, such as happiness and contentment, and can improve our overall well-being.

Helps us to see the bigger picture: Celebrating progress and recognizing accomplishments can help us to see the bigger picture and remind us of why we started working towards our goals in the first place. It can help us to stay focused and motivated towards our long-term objectives.

Tips for celebrating progress and recognizing accomplishments

Set specific goals: To celebrate progress and recognize accomplishments, it's important to have specific goals in mind. These goals should be measurable and achievable, so that you can track your progress and see how far you've come.

Break down larger goals into smaller steps: Breaking down larger goals into smaller, more manageable steps can help you to see progress more easily. Each time you complete a smaller step, celebrate your progress and recognize the accomplishment.

Keep track of your progress: Keep a journal or a list of your accomplishments and progress. This can be a helpful tool to remind you of what you have achieved and how far you've come.

Celebrate all achievements, big and small: Celebrate all of your achievements, no matter how small they may seem. Each accomplishment is a step towards your overall goal, and should be recognized and celebrated.

Share your accomplishments with others: Share your accomplishments with others, such as friends or family. Celebrating with others can make the accomplishment even more meaningful and enjoyable.

Examples of celebrating progress and recognizing accomplishments

Celebrating a promotion: If you receive a promotion at work, celebrate your accomplishment by treating yourself to a special meal or activity. Share the news with your family and friends, and express gratitude towards your colleagues and mentors who helped you along the way.

Completing a difficult task: If you complete a difficult task or project, take a moment to recognize the accomplishment. Treat yourself to a small reward, such as a favorite snack or activity.

Learning a new skill: If you learn a new skill or hobby, celebrate your accomplishment by practicing the skill or hobby and sharing your progress with others. Joining a club or group related to your new skill can also provide a supportive community and a way to celebrate your progress together.

Quiz:

Why is celebrating progress and recognizing accomplishments important?
a. Boosts self-esteem and confidence
b. Provides motivation
c. Encourages gratitude
d. All of the above

What is one tip for celebrating progress and recognizing accomplishments?
a. Set specific goals
b. Reflect on the journey and the process
c. Compare yourself to others
d. Ignore your accomplishments and focus on your shortcomings

What is the difference between celebrating progress and recognizing accomplishments?
a. Celebrating progress focuses on the journey, while recognizing accomplishments focuses on the destination.
b. Celebrating progress focuses on the destination, while recognizing accomplishments focuses on the journey.
c. Celebrating progress and recognizing accomplishments are the same thing.
d. None of the above.

What are some examples of ways to celebrate progress and recognize accomplishments?
a. Throw a party or have a small gathering with friends and family
b. Treat yourself to something you have been wanting or enjoy a nice meal
c. Take a moment to reflect on your journey and give yourself a pat on the back
d. All of the above

What is one benefit of celebrating progress and recognizing accomplishments regularly?
a. Improved mental health and well-being
b. Increased job satisfaction
c. Improved relationships with others
d. All of the above

True or False: Celebrating progress and recognizing accomplishments is only important for big accomplishments, such as graduating college or getting a promotion.
a. True
b. False

CHAPTER 4: NUTRITION AND MENTAL HEALTH:

When it comes to mental health, there are many factors that can influence how we feel and function on a daily basis. While therapy and medication are often seen as the go-to treatments for mental health conditions, there is one aspect that is often overlooked: nutrition. What we put into our bodies can have a profound impact on how we feel, think, and behave.

Research has shown that there is a clear link between what we eat and our mental health. Eating a balanced diet rich in nutrients can help reduce the risk of developing certain mental health conditions, as well as improve symptoms in those who already have them. On the other hand, a poor diet high in processed foods and sugar can contribute to depression, anxiety, and other mental health issues.

In this chapter, we will explore the connection between nutrition and mental health. We will look at the science behind how food affects the brain, as well as practical tips and advice for incorporating healthy eating habits into your life. Whether you are looking to improve your mental health, manage a specific condition, or simply maintain overall well-being, this chapter will provide you with valuable information and resources to help you achieve your goals. So let's dive in and discover the power of nutrition for mental health.

The Gut-Brain Connection

Have you ever experienced feeling anxious or depressed after a meal? Or felt your stomach ache during a stressful situation? These experiences are not uncommon, and they are a result of the gut-brain connection. Our gut and brain are in constant communication, and what we eat can have a significant impact on our mental health. In this chapter, we will explore the gut-brain connection and how our diet can influence our mental well-being. We'll discuss the science behind the connection, common gut issues that affect mental health, and tips on how to maintain a healthy gut through nutrition.

How the Gut and Brain Communicate

Have you ever experienced "butterflies" in your stomach before a big event or felt a sense of unease after eating a certain food? Our gut and brain are more interconnected than we realize. The gut-brain connection, also known as the gut-brain axis, is a complex and fascinating topic that has gained attention in recent years. In this chapter, we will explore how the gut and brain communicate, the role of the vagus nerve and neurotransmitters, and the important role of gut microbes in this process.

The Vagus Nerve

The vagus nerve is the longest cranial nerve in our body, running from the brainstem to the abdomen. It plays a critical role in the gut-brain axis by transmitting information between the brain and the digestive system. The vagus nerve is a two-way communication highway, with signals being sent from the brain to the gut and vice versa.

The vagus nerve has a direct influence on digestion, controlling important processes such as the release of digestive enzymes and the motility of the gut. It also plays a role in regulating our mood and emotions. Studies have shown that stimulating the vagus nerve can help improve symptoms of depression and anxiety.

Neurotransmitters

Neurotransmitters are chemical messengers in the brain that play a crucial role in our mood, behavior, and overall mental health. What many people don't realize is that the majority of neurotransmitters are actually produced in the gut. In fact, over 90% of our body's serotonin, a neurotransmitter that regulates mood and anxiety, is produced in the gut.

The gut also produces other important neurotransmitters such as dopamine and GABA. These neurotransmitters play a role in regulating our appetite, motivation, and even our sleep. When our gut is not functioning properly, it can have a significant impact on our mental health.

The Role of Gut Microbes

The gut is home to trillions of microbes, collectively known as the gut microbiota. These microbes play a critical role in our health, influencing everything from our immune system to our mood. Recent research has shown that the gut microbiota also plays a significant role in the gut-brain axis.

The gut microbiota communicates with the brain through various pathways, including the vagus nerve and the production of neurotransmitters. It can influence our mood and behavior by regulating the levels of certain neurotransmitters, such as serotonin and GABA. Studies have also shown that altering the gut microbiota can have a significant impact on our mental health, with some research suggesting that certain probiotics may be helpful in treating anxiety and depression.

Conclusion:

The gut-brain connection is a complex and fascinating topic that highlights the importance of a healthy gut for our overall mental health. By understanding how the gut and brain communicate, we can take steps to support our gut health and improve our mental well-being. From incorporating probiotics into our diet to practicing relaxation techniques that stimulate the vagus nerve, there are many actionable steps we can take to support the gut-brain axis and improve our quality of life.

Common Gut Issues That Affect Mental Health

Are you feeling anxious or depressed lately? It might surprise you to learn that the root cause of these problems could be in your gut. It might sound strange, but our gut health and our mental health are connected in a complex way. This chapter will explore some common gut issues that can affect your mental health.

Irritable Bowel Syndrome (IBS)

If you experience frequent abdominal pain, bloating, constipation or diarrhea, you might be suffering from Irritable Bowel Syndrome (IBS). IBS is a common gut disorder that affects millions of people worldwide. Studies have shown that people with IBS are more likely to develop depression and anxiety. It's not clear why IBS affects mental health, but it could be due to the gut-brain axis.

Inflammatory Bowel Disease (IBD)

Inflammatory Bowel Disease (IBD) is a group of chronic inflammatory disorders of the gastrointestinal tract. Crohn's disease and ulcerative colitis are two common types of IBD. The symptoms of IBD include abdominal pain, diarrhea, weight loss, and fatigue. People with IBD are at higher risk of developing mental health problems like depression, anxiety, and mood disorders.

Leaky Gut Syndrome

Leaky gut syndrome is a condition in which the lining of the intestine becomes permeable, allowing undigested food particles, toxins, and bacteria to leak into the bloodstream. This can cause an immune response that leads to inflammation throughout the body. The symptoms of leaky gut syndrome can include bloating, gas, diarrhea, fatigue, joint pain, and skin problems. Leaky gut syndrome can also lead to mental health problems like anxiety and depression.

Small Intestinal Bacterial Overgrowth (SIBO)

Small Intestinal Bacterial Overgrowth (SIBO) is a condition in which there is an overgrowth of bacteria in the small intestine. This can lead to malabsorption of nutrients, gas, bloating, and abdominal pain. SIBO has been linked to mental health problems like anxiety, depression, and brain fog.

Gut Dysbiosis

Gut dysbiosis is an imbalance in the gut microbiota, which are the trillions of bacteria that live in our digestive tract. When the balance of good and bad bacteria is disrupted, it can lead to inflammation, food sensitivities, and other digestive problems. Gut dysbiosis has been linked to mental health problems like depression, anxiety, and even autism.

In conclusion, gut health and mental health are closely linked. Common gut issues like IBS, IBD, leaky gut syndrome, SIBO, and gut dysbiosis can all affect mental health. If you are struggling with mental health issues, it's important to consider your gut health as part of the picture. Improving your gut health through diet, lifestyle changes, and supplements can help improve your mental health as well.

The Impact of Nutrition on Mental

When it comes to mental health, most people tend to focus on traditional treatments such as therapy and medication. However, what you eat can also have a significant impact on your mental well-being. Studies have shown that certain foods and dietary patterns can improve mood, reduce symptoms of depression and anxiety, and even prevent mental health conditions. In this chapter, we'll explore the impact of nutrition on mental health, including the Mediterranean diet, the gut-brain connection and its link to depression and anxiety, the importance of probiotics and prebiotics, and foods to avoid for better mental health.

The Mediterranean Diet:

The Mediterranean diet is a way of eating that is based on the traditional cuisine of countries bordering the Mediterranean Sea, such as Greece, Italy, and Spain. It emphasizes whole foods such as fruits, vegetables, whole grains, legumes, nuts, and seeds, as well as healthy fats such as olive oil and fatty fish like salmon. Research has shown that following a Mediterranean-style diet can reduce the risk of depression and improve overall mental health.

One study published in the journal BMC Medicine found that adults who followed a Mediterranean diet for four years had a lower risk of developing depression than those who followed a typical Western diet. Another study published in the Journal of the American Medical Association found that a Mediterranean diet supplemented with nuts and extra-virgin olive oil was associated with a reduced risk of major cardiovascular events, including depression.

- Greek salad
- Hummus
- Tabouli
- Greek yogurt with honey and nuts
- Mediterranean-style grilled fish
- Baked eggplant with tomato and feta cheese
- Chickpea stew with spinach and tomatoes
- Ratatouille
- Tuna and white bean salad
- Grilled chicken kebabs with veggies
- Greek-style lentil soup
- Roasted vegetables with herbs and garlic
- Whole wheat pasta with tomato sauce and olives
- Fruit and nut bars
- Fruit salad with honey and cinnamon

Breakfast:

Greek Yogurt with Honey and Nuts Recipe:

Ingredients:

1 cup plain Greek yogurt
1 tablespoon honey
1/4 cup mixed nuts (such as almonds, walnuts, and pistachios), chopped
Instructions:

In a small bowl, mix together the Greek yogurt and honey until well combined.
Top the yogurt with the chopped nuts.
Serve immediately and enjoy!
Nutritional Information (per serving):

Calories: 279
Fat: 14g
Carbohydrates: 19g
Fiber: 1g
Protein: 20g
Note: Nutritional information may vary depending on the specific brands and quantities of ingredients used.

Lunch

Roasted Vegetables with Herbs and Garlic:

Ingredients:

1 large sweet potato, peeled and diced
2 cups Brussels sprouts, trimmed and halved
1 red bell pepper, seeded and chopped
1 yellow bell pepper, seeded and chopped
1 red onion, peeled and cut into wedges
3 garlic cloves, minced
2 tablespoons olive oil
1 teaspoon dried thyme
1 teaspoon dried oregano
Salt and pepper, to taste
Instructions:

Preheat your oven to 425°F.

In a large mixing bowl, combine the diced sweet potato, halved Brussels sprouts, chopped red and yellow bell peppers, and onion wedges.

In a separate small bowl, whisk together the minced garlic, olive oil, dried thyme, dried oregano, salt, and pepper until well combined.

Pour the garlic and herb mixture over the vegetables and toss until evenly coated.

Spread the vegetables out in a single layer on a large baking sheet.

Roast the vegetables in the preheated oven for 25-30 minutes, or until they are tender and lightly browned, stirring once halfway through cooking.

Remove the vegetables from the oven and serve hot.
Nutrition Facts (per serving):

Calories: 148
Fat: 6g
Carbohydrates: 22g

Fiber: 6g
Protein: 4g
Sodium: 69mg

Note: This recipe serves 4 people as a side dish. You can adjust the ingredients and serving size as needed to fit your dietary needs.

Dinner

Ratatouille:

Ingredients:

1 large eggplant, chopped into 1-inch pieces
2 medium zucchinis, chopped into 1-inch pieces
1 large onion, chopped
1 red bell pepper, chopped into 1-inch pieces
1 yellow bell pepper, chopped into 1-inch pieces
4 cloves garlic, minced
1 can (28 oz) crushed tomatoes
2 tbsp tomato paste
1 tsp dried thyme
1 tsp dried oregano
Salt and pepper, to taste
2 tbsp olive oil
Fresh basil, chopped, for garnish

Instructions:

Preheat oven to 375°F.

In a large bowl, mix together the eggplant, zucchini, onion, bell peppers, garlic, olive oil, thyme, oregano, salt, and pepper.

Spread the vegetables evenly on a large baking sheet.

Bake for 35-40 minutes, or until the vegetables are tender and lightly browned.

In a large saucepan, heat the crushed tomatoes, tomato paste, and a pinch of salt and pepper.

Add the roasted vegetables to the tomato sauce and stir to combine.

Simmer for 10-15 minutes to allow the flavors to meld.

Serve hot, garnished with fresh chopped basil.

Nutritional information (per serving, makes 4 servings):

Calories: 150
Fat: 6g
Carbohydrates: 22g
Protein: 5g
Fiber: 8g
Sugar: 13g
Sodium: 340mg

The Gut-Brain Connection and Depression:

The gut-brain connection refers to the complex bidirectional communication between the gut and the brain. The gut is home to trillions of bacteria, collectively known as the gut microbiome. These bacteria play a crucial role in regulating the immune system, producing neurotransmitters, and maintaining the integrity of the gut lining. When the gut microbiome is disrupted, it can lead to a range of health problems, including depression.

Research has shown that individuals with depression have different gut microbiome composition than healthy individuals. Specifically, they have lower levels of certain beneficial bacteria, such as Bifidobacterium and Lactobacillus. Probiotics, which are live microorganisms that confer a health benefit, have been shown to improve symptoms of depression by restoring the balance of the gut microbiome.

The Gut-Brain Connection and Anxiety:

Anxiety disorders are among the most common mental health conditions worldwide. Like depression, anxiety has been linked to disruptions in the gut microbiome. In particular, research has shown that individuals with anxiety have lower levels of the anti-inflammatory cytokine interleukin-10, which is produced by the gut microbiome.

One study published in the journal Psychiatry Research found that individuals with generalized anxiety disorder who took a probiotic supplement for four weeks had reduced symptoms of anxiety compared to those who took a placebo. Other studies have shown that prebiotics, which are non-digestible fibers that promote the growth of beneficial gut bacteria, can also improve symptoms of anxiety.

The Importance of Probiotics and Prebiotics:

Probiotics and prebiotics are two types of dietary fibers that can promote a healthy gut microbiome. Probiotics are live microorganisms that are found in fermented foods such as yogurt, kefir, sauerkraut, and kimchi. Prebiotics, on the other hand, are non-digestible fibers that are found in foods such as onions, garlic, asparagus, and bananas.

Studies have shown that probiotics and prebiotics can improve mental health outcomes, including reducing symptoms of depression and anxiety. However, it's important to note that not all probiotics and prebiotics are created equal. Different strains of probiotics have different effects on the gut microbiome, and some prebiotics can be difficult to digest and can cause

There are many foods that can help improve mental health. Here are some examples:

Fatty fish: Fatty fish like salmon, tuna, and sardines are rich in omega-3 fatty acids, which are essential for brain health and can help reduce symptoms of depression and anxiety.

Nuts and seeds: Nuts and seeds like almonds, walnuts, flaxseeds, and chia seeds are high in healthy fats, fiber, and antioxidants, which can improve brain function and reduce inflammation.

Leafy greens: Leafy greens like spinach, kale, and Swiss chard are rich in vitamins and minerals like folate, which can improve mood and reduce symptoms of depression.

Whole grains: Whole grains like brown rice, quinoa, and oats are high in fiber, which can help regulate mood and reduce symptoms of anxiety.

Fermented foods: Fermented foods like yogurt, kefir, and sauerkraut are high in probiotics, which can improve gut health and reduce symptoms of depression and anxiety.

Berries: Berries like blueberries, raspberries, and strawberries are high in antioxidants, which can improve brain function and reduce inflammation.

Dark chocolate: Dark chocolate is high in antioxidants and can improve mood and reduce symptoms of depression and anxiety when consumed in moderation.

It's important to note that while these foods can be helpful for mental health, they should be part of a balanced diet that includes a variety of fruits, vegetables, whole grains, and lean proteins.

Breakfast:

Blueberry and Almond Butter Overnight Oats

Ingredients:

1/2 cup rolled oats
1/2 cup almond milk
1/4 cup plain Greek yogurt
1/4 cup fresh or frozen blueberries
1 tablespoon chia seeds
1 tablespoon almond butter
1/2 teaspoon vanilla extract
Optional toppings: sliced almonds, additional blueberries

Nutrition Facts:
Serving size: 1 serving
Calories: 377
Total Fat: 20g
Saturated Fat: 3g
Cholesterol: 0mg
Sodium: 99mg
Total Carbohydrates: 41g
Dietary Fiber: 11g
Sugar: 9g
Protein: 12g

Please note that this is an estimate and may vary based on the specific ingredients and brands used in the recipe.

Directions:

In a small bowl or jar, combine the rolled oats, almond milk, Greek yogurt, blueberries, chia seeds, almond butter, and vanilla extract. Stir until well combined.

Cover and refrigerate overnight, or for at least 4 hours.

In the morning, stir the oats and top with sliced almonds and additional blueberries, if desired. Enjoy!

This recipe is packed with mood-boosting ingredients. Blueberries are a good source of antioxidants, which help reduce inflammation in the brain and improve mood. Almond butter is high in healthy fats and protein, which can help stabilize blood sugar levels and improve energy and mood. Chia seeds are a good source of fiber, which can also help regulate blood sugar levels and improve mood. Plus, the combination of creamy almond butter and juicy blueberries makes for a delicious and satisfying breakfast.

Lunch:

Mediterranean Quinoa Salad

Ingredients:

1 cup quinoa
2 cups vegetable broth or water
1 can chickpeas, drained and rinsed
1 cup cherry tomatoes, halved
1 small cucumber, diced
1/2 red onion, diced
1/4 cup Kalamata olives, chopped
1/4 cup feta cheese, crumbled
2 tablespoons chopped fresh parsley
2 tablespoons chopped fresh mint
2 tablespoons lemon juice
2 tablespoons olive oil
Salt and pepper to taste

nutritional information:

Calories: 450
Protein: 23g
Carbohydrates: 40g
Fiber: 12g
Sugar: 7g
Fat: 23g
Saturated Fat: 3g
Cholesterol: 0mg
Sodium: 440mg
Note that the nutritional information may vary based on the specific ingredients and quantities used.

Instructions:

Rinse the quinoa in a fine mesh strainer and transfer to a medium-sized saucepan. Add the vegetable broth or water and bring to a boil over high heat.

Reduce the heat to low and cover the saucepan. Simmer for 15-20 minutes, or until the quinoa is tender and the liquid is absorbed. Remove from heat and let cool.

In a large bowl, combine the cooked quinoa, chickpeas, cherry tomatoes, cucumber, red onion, olives, feta cheese, parsley, and mint.

In a small bowl, whisk together the lemon juice, olive oil, salt, and pepper. Pour the dressing over the quinoa mixture and toss to coat.

Serve immediately or chill in the refrigerator for a few hours before serving.

This recipe serves 4 and each serving provides approximately 370 calories, 14g of protein, 14g of fat, and 50g of carbohydrates. Quinoa is a great source of protein and fiber, while the vegetables provide important vitamins and minerals. The olive oil and feta cheese add healthy fats, and the fresh herbs and lemon juice provide a burst of flavor.

Dinner:

Garlic and Herb Grilled Chicken with Quinoa Salad

Ingredients:

4 boneless, skinless chicken breasts
2 tablespoons olive oil
1 tablespoon minced garlic
1 tablespoon chopped fresh thyme
1 tablespoon chopped fresh rosemary
Salt and pepper
1 cup quinoa
2 cups water
1/4 cup chopped fresh parsley
1/4 cup chopped fresh mint
1/2 cup cherry tomatoes, halved
1/2 cup chopped cucumber
1/4 cup chopped red onion
Juice of 1 lemon
2 tablespoons olive oil
Instructions:

Preheat grill to medium-high heat.

In a small bowl, mix together olive oil, garlic, thyme, rosemary, salt, and pepper.

Brush chicken breasts with the mixture and grill for 5-7 minutes on each side, until fully cooked.

While the chicken is cooking, rinse quinoa in a fine mesh strainer and combine with 2 cups of water in a medium saucepan. Bring to a boil, then reduce heat to low and simmer for 15-20 minutes, until quinoa is cooked and fluffy.

In a large bowl, combine cooked quinoa, parsley, mint, cherry tomatoes, cucumber, and red onion.

In a small bowl, whisk together lemon juice and olive oil to make a dressing.

Pour the dressing over the quinoa salad and toss to combine.
Serve the grilled chicken on top of the quinoa salad.
Nutritional Information (per serving):

Calories: 439
Protein: 37g
Fat: 20g
Carbohydrates: 30g
Fiber: 4g
Sugar: 2g
Sodium: 110mg

This dish is packed with protein from the grilled chicken and quinoa, and also includes plenty of fresh vegetables and herbs for added nutrients. The healthy fats from the olive oil and herbs can also help improve mood and reduce inflammation in the body.

Sweet Potato and Black Bean Salad

Ingredients:

2 medium sweet potatoes, peeled and diced
1 can of black beans, drained and rinsed
1 red bell pepper, diced
1/2 red onion, diced
1/4 cup chopped cilantro
2 tablespoons olive oil
1 tablespoon lime juice
Salt and pepper to taste
Optional: avocado for topping
Instructions:

Preheat oven to 400°F.

Toss diced sweet potatoes in olive oil and spread out on a baking sheet. Roast for 20-25 minutes, or until tender and slightly browned.

In a large bowl, combine roasted sweet potatoes, black beans, diced red bell pepper, diced red onion, and chopped cilantro.

Drizzle lime juice over the mixture and toss to coat.

Season with salt and pepper to taste.

Top with sliced avocado if desired.

Nutritional information (per serving):
Calories: 338
Protein: 10g
Fat: 12g
Carbohydrates: 51g
Fiber: 12g
Sugar: 7g
Sodium: 273mg

This salad is high in fiber and antioxidants, and the sweet potatoes provide complex carbohydrates that can help regulate blood sugar levels and stabilize mood. The black beans are a good source of protein and also contain tryptophan, an amino acid that can help boost serotonin levels in the brain.

Chopped Veggie Salad with Citrus Dressing

Ingredients:

2 cups chopped mixed vegetables (such as cucumber, bell pepper, carrot, radish, and celery)
1/2 cup chopped cherry tomatoes
1/4 cup chopped red onion
1/4 cup chopped fresh parsley
1/4 cup chopped fresh cilantro
1/4 cup chopped fresh mint
2 tbsp. chopped walnuts or almonds
2 tbsp. pumpkin seeds
1 tbsp. hemp seeds
Juice of 1 lemon
Juice of 1 orange
1 tbsp. extra-virgin olive oil
1 tsp. honey or maple syrup
Salt and pepper, to taste
Directions:

In a large bowl, combine the chopped vegetables, cherry tomatoes, red onion, parsley, cilantro, and mint.

In a separate bowl, whisk together the lemon juice, orange juice, olive oil, honey/maple syrup, and salt and pepper.

Pour the dressing over the vegetable mixture and toss until well coated.

Top the salad with the chopped nuts and seeds.

Serve immediately or chill in the fridge for a refreshing and satisfying lunch.

Nutritional information (per serving):

Calories: 210
Total fat: 16g
Saturated fat: 2g
Cholesterol: 0mg
Sodium: 45mg
Total carbohydrates: 16g
Dietary fiber: 5g
Sugars: 7g
Protein: 6g
Vitamin D: 0%
Calcium: 7%
Iron: 14%
Potassium: 10%

Decadent Dessert

Chocolate Avocado Mousse

Ingredients:

2 ripe avocados
1/4 cup cocoa powder
1/4 cup maple syrup
1/4 cup almond milk
1 tsp vanilla extract
1/4 tsp sea salt
Optional toppings: chopped nuts, sliced fruit, shredded coconut
Instructions:

Cut the avocados in half, remove the pit, and scoop out the flesh into a food processor or blender.
Add the cocoa powder, maple syrup, almond milk, vanilla extract, and sea salt to the food processor or blender.
Blend the mixture until it is completely smooth and creamy.
Spoon the chocolate avocado mousse into serving dishes.
Optional: top with chopped nuts, sliced fruit, or shredded coconut.
Refrigerate for at least 30 minutes to chill the mousse and allow the flavors to meld together.
Enjoy!
This dessert is not only delicious, but it is also packed with mood-boosting ingredients. Avocados are high in healthy fats and B vitamins, which can help support brain function and reduce symptoms of depression and anxiety. Cocoa powder is rich in flavonoids, which have been shown to improve mood and cognitive function. Maple syrup contains antioxidants and minerals that can help reduce inflammation and support overall health. And almonds are high in magnesium, which can help regulate mood and reduce stress.

Calories: 292
Protein: 6g
Fat: 22g
Saturated Fat: 7g
Carbohydrates: 28g
Fiber: 9g
Sugar: 13g
Sodium: 79mg

Please note that these are rough estimates and may vary slightly based on the specific ingredients and brands used.

For more recipes to help with mood and diet pick up "Cooking with the Stars and Stripes" A collection of my family favorites an few meals that I have came up with to fit dietary needs of family members,

Journal Exercises:

Write about a time when you noticed a correlation between what you ate and how you felt mentally. How did certain foods make you feel?

_____
_____
_____
_____
_____
_____
_____
_____
_____
_____
_____
_____
_____
_____
_____
_____
_____
_____

Were there any foods that you found made you feel worse?

_____
_____
_____
_____
_____
_____

Make a list of five healthy meals that you enjoy eating. Write about how you feel after eating each one. Do they make you feel energized and alert, or do you feel sluggish and tired?

Write about a time when you turned to food to cope with stress or emotions. How did this affect your mood?

Did it help or make things worse?

Quiz:

True or false: The gut and the brain communicate with each other through the vagus nerve.

Which of the following foods is a good source of probiotics?
a. White bread
b. Yogurt
c. French fries
d. Potato chips

True or false: The Mediterranean diet has been shown to improve mental health outcomes.

What is a common gut issue that can affect mental health?
a. Arthritis
b. Psoriasis
c. Irritable bowel syndrome (IBS)
d. Migraines

Survey:

On a scale of 1-10, how important do you think nutrition is for mental health?
How often do you eat a meal that includes a variety of fruits and vegetables?
a. Multiple times a day
b. Once a day
c. A few times a week
d. Rarely
Have you ever noticed a correlation between what you eat and how you feel mentally? If yes, please describe.
Do you believe that changing your diet could improve your mental health?
a. Yes, significantly
b. Yes, somewhat

c. No, not really
d. No, not at all.

CHAPTER 5: SLEEP AND MENTAL HEALTH

Have you ever had a terrible night's sleep and woken up feeling groggy and irritable? Or maybe you've experienced a prolonged period of poor sleep, leaving you feeling exhausted and unable to function properly. If so, you know firsthand the impact that lack of sleep can have on your mental health.

Sleep is essential for our well-being. It allows our bodies to repair and recharge, and it's crucial for maintaining healthy brain function. Unfortunately, many people struggle to get the recommended seven to nine hours of sleep each night.

In this chapter, we'll explore the vital connection between sleep and mental health. We'll examine how sleep affects our mood, cognition, and overall mental well-being. We'll also provide practical tips for improving sleep hygiene and recognizing and managing sleep disorders.

You'll learn how simple changes to your daily routine can help you get a better night's sleep, including tips on creating a comfortable sleep environment, establishing a consistent bedtime routine, and avoiding common sleep disruptors such as caffeine and electronics.

We'll also dive into the most common sleep disorders, including insomnia, sleep apnea, and restless leg syndrome. You'll discover their symptoms, causes, and effective treatment options.

To further illustrate the impact of sleep on mental health, we'll share stories of individuals who have improved their mental health by prioritizing sleep. You'll see firsthand how small changes can have a significant impact on overall well-being.

By the end of this chapter, you'll have a newfound appreciation for the importance of sleep and the role it plays in your mental health. You'll be equipped with practical tools to improve your sleep hygiene and recognize and manage sleep disorders. So, let's dive in and discover the power of a good night's sleep.

Tips for improving sleep hygiene

Getting enough sleep is essential for good mental health. Unfortunately, many people struggle to get the recommended 7-9 hours of sleep per night. If you're one of them, don't worry - there are many things you can do to improve your sleep hygiene and get the restful sleep you need. In this chapter, we'll explore some tips and tricks to help you improve your sleep hygiene and get a better night's sleep.

Stick to a consistent sleep schedule

One of the best things you can do to improve your sleep hygiene is to stick to a consistent sleep schedule. Go to bed and wake up at the same time every day, even on weekends. This will help regulate your body's natural sleep-wake cycle, making it easier to fall asleep and wake up feeling refreshed.

Create a relaxing bedtime routine

Establishing a relaxing bedtime routine can help signal to your body that it's time to wind down and prepare for sleep. This could include taking a warm bath, reading a book, or doing some gentle stretching or yoga. Avoid screens and bright lights in the hour leading up to bedtime, as these can disrupt your body's production of melatonin, a hormone that helps regulate sleep.

Create a sleep-conducive environment

Your sleep environment can have a big impact on the quality of your sleep. Make sure your bedroom is cool, dark, and quiet. Use blackout curtains or a sleep mask to block out any light, and consider using earplugs or white noise if you're sensitive to sound. Invest in a comfortable mattress and pillows that support your sleeping position.

Limit caffeine and alcohol

Caffeine is a stimulant that can interfere with sleep, so it's best to avoid it in the hours leading up to bedtime. Similarly, while alcohol may help you fall asleep initially, it can disrupt your sleep later in the night, leading to poorer sleep quality overall. Try to limit your caffeine intake to the morning and early afternoon, and avoid drinking alcohol in the hours before bed.

Get regular exercise

Regular exercise has been shown to improve sleep quality, so make sure you're getting enough physical activity each day. Aim for at least 30 minutes of moderate exercise most days of the week. Just make sure to avoid vigorous exercise in the hours leading up to bedtime, as this can make it harder to fall asleep.

Manage stress

Stress and anxiety can make it difficult to fall asleep and stay asleep. Find healthy ways to manage stress, such as practicing mindfulness, deep breathing, or yoga. Consider talking to a mental health professional if you're struggling with persistent stress or anxiety.

Avoid daytime napping

While napping can be tempting, especially if you're feeling tired during the day, it can interfere with your ability to fall asleep and stay asleep at night. If you must nap, limit it to 20-30 minutes and avoid napping later in the day.

By incorporating these tips into your daily routine, you can improve your sleep hygiene and get the restful, restorative sleep you need for good mental health. Remember, getting enough sleep isn't a luxury - it's a necessity. Prioritize your sleep, and you'll be rewarded with better mental and physical health.

Sleep Hygiene Worksheet

How many hours of sleep do you typically get each night?

What time do you usually go to bed at night?

What time do you usually wake up in the morning?

Do you feel well-rested when you wake up in the morning? Yes/No

Do you have trouble falling asleep at night? Yes/No

Do you have trouble staying asleep during the night? Yes/No

Do you feel tired or groggy during the day? Yes/No

Do you take naps during the day? Yes/No

How many caffeinated beverages do you consume per day?

a. None
b. 1-2
c. 3-4
d. 5 or more

How much alcohol do you consume per week?
a. None

b. 1-2 drinks
c. 3-4 drinks
d. 5 or more drinks

How often do you exercise per week?
a. Never
b. 1-2 times per week
c. 3-4 times per week
d. 5 or more times per week

How many hours before bed do you eat your last meal?
a. Less than 1 hour
b. 1-2 hours
c. 3-4 hours
d. More than 4 hours

How many hours before bed do you consume caffeine?
a. Less than 1 hour
b. 1-2 hours
c. 3-4 hours
d. More than 4 hours

How many hours before bed do you consume alcohol?
a. Less than 1 hour
b. 1-2 hours
c. 3-4 hours
d. More than 4 hours

How many hours before bed do you exercise?
a. Less than 1 hour
b. 1-2 hours
c. 3-4 hours
d. More than 4 hours

Do you have a consistent bedtime routine? Yes/No

What do you typically do before bed?

a. Watch TV
b. Use your phone or other electronic devices
c. Read a book
d. Take a bath or shower
e. Other (write in)

What is the temperature like in your bedroom?
a. Too hot
b. Too cold
c. Just right

Do you have a comfortable mattress and pillows? Yes/No

Do you have any sleep aids that you use? Yes/No

Do you have a quiet, dark, and peaceful sleep environment? Yes/No

How do you deal with stress before bedtime?

a. Meditate or do relaxation exercises
b. Write in a journal
c. Practice deep breathing techniques
d. Talk to someone
e. Other (write in)

Have you ever tried any natural remedies to help you sleep? Yes/No

Have you ever talked to a healthcare professional about your sleep problems? Yes/No

What changes can you make to improve your sleep hygiene?

a. Go to bed at a consistent time each night
b. Create a relaxing bedtime routine

c. Avoid caffeine, alcohol, and heavy meals before bedtime
d. Make your sleep environment comfortable and peaceful
e. Other (write in)

Sleep disorders are a common issue that can have a significant impact on mental health. According to the National Sleep Foundation, more than 50 million Americans suffer from a sleep disorder. Sleep disorders can include difficulty falling asleep, staying asleep, or waking up too early, as well as problems with the quality of sleep.

If you are experiencing any of these issues, it is important to recognize the signs of sleep disorders and seek help if needed. Here are some common sleep disorders and how to manage them:

Insomnia: Insomnia is a sleep disorder characterized by difficulty falling or staying asleep. It can be caused by stress, anxiety, depression, or other factors. To manage insomnia, it is important to establish a regular sleep routine and create a relaxing sleep environment. Avoiding caffeine, alcohol, and heavy meals before bedtime can also help.

Sleep Apnea: Sleep apnea is a sleep disorder characterized by pauses in breathing or shallow breathing during sleep. It can be caused by obesity, smoking, or other factors. To manage sleep apnea, it is important to seek medical treatment, which may include the use of a continuous positive airway pressure (CPAP) machine.

Restless Leg Syndrome: Restless leg syndrome is a sleep disorder characterized by an uncontrollable urge to move the legs, especially at night. It can be caused by iron deficiency, pregnancy, or other factors. To manage restless leg syndrome, it is important to establish a regular sleep routine, take a warm bath before bedtime, and avoid caffeine and alcohol.

Narcolepsy: Narcolepsy is a sleep disorder characterized by excessive daytime sleepiness and sudden sleep attacks. It can be caused by a genetic disorder or a problem with the brain's ability to regulate sleep. To manage narcolepsy, it is important to seek medical treatment, which may include the use of medications such as stimulants.

Parasomnias: Parasomnias are sleep disorders that involve abnormal movements, behaviors, emotions, perceptions, or dreams during sleep. Examples of parasomnias include sleepwalking, nightmares, and night terrors. To manage parasomnias, it is important to establish a regular sleep routine, create a relaxing sleep environment, and avoid alcohol and drugs that can disrupt sleep.

It is important to seek medical help if you are experiencing any of these sleep disorders. In addition, making lifestyle changes such as establishing a regular sleep routine, creating a relaxing sleep environment, and avoiding caffeine, alcohol, and heavy meals before bedtime can help improve the quality of your sleep.

In conclusion, sleep disorders can have a significant impact on mental health, but with the right treatment and lifestyle changes, they can be managed. It is important to recognize the signs of sleep disorders and seek help if needed to improve the quality of your sleep and overall mental health.

Quiz

What is insomnia?
a. A sleep disorder characterized by excessive sleepiness during the day.
b. A sleep disorder characterized by difficulty falling or staying asleep.
c. A sleep disorder characterized by sudden and uncontrollable sleep attacks.

What is sleep apnea?
a. A sleep disorder characterized by excessive sleepiness during the day.
b. A sleep disorder characterized by difficulty falling or staying asleep.

c. A sleep disorder characterized by pauses in breathing or shallow breathing during sleep.

What is restless leg syndrome?
a. A sleep disorder characterized by excessive sleepiness during the day.
b. A sleep disorder characterized by difficulty falling or staying asleep.
c. A sleep disorder characterized by uncomfortable sensations in the legs, particularly at night, that often result in an irresistible urge to move them.

What is narcolepsy?
a. A sleep disorder characterized by excessive sleepiness during the day.
b. A sleep disorder characterized by difficulty falling or staying asleep.
c. A sleep disorder characterized by sudden and uncontrollable sleep attacks.

Which of the following is NOT a common treatment for sleep disorders?
a. Medications
b. Cognitive-behavioral therapy
c. Surgery
d. Home remedies like drinking warm milk before bed

How is sleep apnea diagnosed?
a. A sleep study that measures brain waves, eye movements, and heart rate during sleep.
b. Blood tests.
c. A physical exam.

What are some common risk factors for sleep apnea?
a. Being overweight or obese.
b. Being a smoker.
c. Having a family history of sleep apnea.
d. All of the above.

What is the recommended amount of sleep for adults?
a. 4-5 hours per night.

b. 6-7 hours per night.
c. 8-9 hours per night.

What are some potential consequences of untreated sleep disorders?
a. High blood pressure
b. Diabetes
c. Depression
d. All of the above.

What can you do to improve your sleep hygiene?
a. Stick to a regular sleep schedule.
b. Create a relaxing bedtime routine.
c. Avoid caffeine, alcohol, and heavy meals before bedtime.
d. Keep your bedroom quiet, dark, and cool.
e. All of the above.

CHAPTER 6: LIFESTYLE CHANGES FOR A POSITIVE MINDSET

Welcome to Chapter 6: Lifestyle Changes for a Positive Mindset! In this chapter, we will discuss the power of exercise, nutrition, and sleep in improving our mental health. Our physical and mental health are intricately connected, and making positive changes in one area can have a significant impact on the other.

Exercise has been shown to release endorphins, which are natural mood-boosters that can reduce feelings of stress and anxiety. Additionally, regular exercise can improve sleep quality, increase energy levels, and enhance overall physical health. Nutrition is also a crucial component of mental health. Eating a balanced diet that includes plenty of fruits, vegetables, whole grains, and lean proteins can provide the nutrients our brains need to function at their best.

And, of course, we can't forget about the importance of sleep. Getting enough high-quality sleep is essential for maintaining good mental health. Lack of sleep can lead to irritability, difficulty concentrating, and mood swings, among other negative effects.

But making lifestyle changes can be challenging, especially when we have busy schedules and competing priorities. That's why in this chapter, we'll provide you with practical tips for making sustainable lifestyle changes that can help you feel better both physically and mentally. We'll also share stories of real people who have successfully made lifestyle changes to improve their mental health.

By the end of this chapter, you'll have the knowledge and tools you need to make positive changes in your own life. Whether you're looking to reduce stress, boost your mood, or simply feel better overall, this chapter will provide you with the guidance and inspiration you need to get started. So let's dive in!

Discuss how exercise, nutrition, and sleep work together to improve mental health

When it comes to improving mental health, many people focus solely on therapy and medication. However, there are other aspects of our daily lives that can play a huge role in our mental wellbeing. In particular, exercise, nutrition, and sleep are three interconnected areas that can work together to help boost mood, reduce stress, and improve overall mental health.

Exercise is one of the most well-known ways to improve mental health, but many people may not realize just how beneficial it can be. Studies have shown that exercise can help reduce symptoms of anxiety and depression, increase self-esteem, and improve cognitive function. This is because exercise increases the production of endorphins, which are natural chemicals in the brain that promote feelings of happiness and wellbeing.

Nutrition is another important aspect of mental health that is often overlooked. What we eat can have a profound effect on our mood and energy levels. Eating a diet high in whole, nutrient-dense foods can help improve mental clarity, reduce inflammation, and increase feelings of overall wellbeing. On the other hand, consuming highly processed foods and sugary drinks can have the opposite effect, leading to feelings of fatigue, mood swings, and even depression.

Finally, sleep is crucial for both physical and mental health. Lack of sleep has been linked to a range of mental health issues, including anxiety, depression, and even bipolar disorder. This is because sleep plays a vital role in regulating our mood and emotional state. When we don't get enough sleep, our emotional regulation can be compromised, leading to heightened anxiety and stress.

By focusing on exercise, nutrition, and sleep together, we can create a powerful trio that can help improve mental health in a holistic and sustainable way. Rather than relying solely on medication or therapy, making lifestyle changes can help support and enhance those treatments.

In the following sections, we will explore each of these areas in more detail, discussing the specific ways in which they can improve mental health, as well as providing practical tips for incorporating these changes into your daily life. We will also share inspiring stories from people who have made these lifestyle changes and experienced significant improvements in their mental health. So, let's get started!

Tips for making sustainable lifestyle changes

- Start small: Make gradual changes that you can maintain in the long term.

- Identify your motivators: Determine what inspires you to make positive changes in your life.

- Set goals: Create specific, measurable, achievable, relevant, and time-bound (SMART) goals.

- Keep track of your progress: Monitor your progress and celebrate your achievements.

- Focus on your strengths: Use your strengths to help you achieve your goals.

- Find an accountability partner: Ask a friend or family member to hold you accountable for your goals.

- Make a plan: Create a plan to help you achieve your goals.

- Create healthy habits: Establish healthy habits, such as eating nutritious foods and exercising regularly.

- Learn to cope with stress: Use healthy coping mechanisms, such as meditation, to manage stress.

- Practice gratitude: Cultivate a sense of gratitude to improve your mental health.

- Get enough sleep: Make sure you get enough sleep to support your physical and mental health.

- Manage your time: Manage your time effectively to reduce stress and improve productivity.

- Surround yourself with positive influences: Surround yourself with people who support and encourage you.

- Practice mindfulness: Use mindfulness techniques, such as deep breathing, to improve your mental well-being.

- Stay hydrated: Drink plenty of water to stay hydrated and support your overall health.

- Create a supportive environment: Make sure your environment is conducive to healthy habits.

- Keep things simple: Simplify your life to reduce stress and make room for positive changes.

- Learn to say no: Set boundaries and learn to say no when necessary to reduce stress and maintain balance.

- Make time for self-care: Take time to care for yourself and engage in activities that bring you joy.

- Cultivate resilience: Learn to bounce back from setbacks and challenges.

- Find healthy ways to socialize: Connect with others in healthy ways, such as through exercise or hobbies.

- Get outside: Spend time in nature to improve your mood and reduce stress.

- Be kind to yourself: Practice self-compassion and be kind to yourself.

- Stay committed: Stay committed to your goals, even when things get tough.

- Keep learning: Stay curious and continue to learn new things to support your growth and well-being.

Mindfulness meditation can be a helpful practice for improving mental health and promoting a positive mindset. Here is a brief guide on how to practice mindfulness meditation:

- Find a quiet and comfortable place to sit or lie down. You can also practice mindfulness while doing activities such as walking or eating, but it's helpful to start with a quiet setting.

- Set a timer for a desired length of time, such as 5 or 10 minutes.

- Close your eyes or focus your gaze on a specific point.

- Take a few deep breaths, inhaling through your nose and exhaling through your mouth.

- Begin to focus your attention on your breath. Notice the sensation of the air moving in and out of your nose or mouth.

- If your mind begins to wander, simply notice the thought without judgment and gently bring your attention back to your breath.

- You can also practice body scan meditation, which involves bringing your attention to different parts of your body and noticing any sensations without judgment.

- As you continue to practice mindfulness meditation, you may find it helpful to use guided meditations or attend a meditation group or class.

Remember, mindfulness meditation is a practice, and it takes time and consistency to develop. Don't judge yourself if you find it difficult at first, and keep practicing regularly to reap the benefits.

Recommended books on personal development that you can check out:

"The 7 Habits of Highly Effective People" by Stephen Covey: This classic book teaches readers how to cultivate positive habits that lead to success in both personal and professional life.

"The Power of Now" by Eckhart Tolle: This book encourages readers to live in the present moment and to let go of negative thoughts and emotions that hold them back from achieving their goals.

"Mindset: The New Psychology of Success" by Carol S. Dweck: This book explores the concept of growth mindset, which is the belief that intelligence and abilities can be developed through hard work and dedication.

"Atomic Habits" by James Clear: This book provides practical tips and strategies for building positive habits and breaking negative ones, leading to a more fulfilling life.

"The Four Agreements" by Don Miguel Ruiz: This book presents four simple principles for living a happy and fulfilling life based on ancient Toltec wisdom.

"The Untethered Soul" by Michael A. Singer: This book helps readers learn to let go of negative thoughts and emotions, so they can experience more peace and happiness in their lives.

"Daring Greatly" by Brené Brown: This book encourages readers to be vulnerable and to embrace their imperfections, leading to more meaningful connections with others and a greater sense of self-worth.

"The Alchemist" by Paulo Coelho: This inspiring novel tells the story of a shepherd boy on a journey of self-discovery and fulfillment, encouraging readers to follow their dreams and live their best life.

Congratulations on completing this book on improving your mindset and mental health! Throughout this journey, we have explored various strategies that can help you build a positive mindset and improve your mental health. We have discussed the importance of self-care, mindfulness, positive self-talk, and developing a growth mindset. But, what we have not yet covered is the crucial role of physical health in improving mental health.

Physical health and mental health are deeply interconnected. When we take care of our bodies, we are also taking care of our minds. Exercise, nutrition, and sleep are all essential components of maintaining good mental health. Exercise releases endorphins that help us feel good, while good nutrition and restful sleep provide the energy and clarity we need to face life's challenges.

As you continue on your journey of personal growth and development, we encourage you to make a commitment to improving your physical health as well. This can be done by making small changes to your diet, starting an exercise routine, and practicing good sleep hygiene. By taking care of your physical health, you will also be taking care of your mental health, and you will feel more empowered to face life's challenges with resilience and positivity.

Remember, personal development is a journey, not a destination. There will be ups and downs along the way, but with persistence and dedication, you can continue to grow and thrive. We hope that this book has provided you with the inspiration and resources to start your journey towards a positive mindset and improved mental health.

If you would like to continue your personal development journey, we recommend checking out some of the recommended books and resources we have provided throughout the book. Additionally, seeking support from a mental health professional can also be a great way to further your personal growth and development.

We wish you all the best on your journey towards a positive mindset and improved mental health. Remember to be kind to yourself, practice self-care, and embrace a growth mindset. With these tools in your toolkit, you can conquer anything that comes your way!

ANSWER KEYS

Quiz Page 55
B) Neurotransmission
C) Jogging
B) Endorphins
C) Increased likelihood of weight gain
A) True

Quiz page 78

Some common psychological reactions to life-changing events include shock, denial, anger, sadness, anxiety, and confusion.

True. Seeking professional help, such as therapy or counseling, can be an important step in coping with the impact of life-changing events on mental health.

Self-care techniques that can help improve mental health after a life-changing event include exercise, meditation, spending time with loved ones, seeking social support, and practicing relaxation techniques.

Strategies for developing resilience after adversity include cultivating positive beliefs about oneself, maintaining healthy relationships, developing coping skills, seeking support, and practicing self-compassion.

Setting realistic goals after a life-changing event is important because it can help individuals feel a sense of control and progress in their lives, which can contribute to a greater sense of well-being and improved mental health.

Quiz page 92

What is the purpose of mindfulness practices and meditation?
The purpose of mindfulness practices and meditation is to cultivate present-moment awareness and develop a non-judgmental acceptance of one's thoughts, emotions, and sensations.

How can mindfulness and meditation benefit our mental and physical health?
Mindfulness and meditation have been found to reduce stress and anxiety, improve sleep quality, enhance mood and emotional regulation, increase focus and concentration, and even lower blood pressure and improve cardiovascular health.

What are some common techniques used in mindfulness and meditation practices?
Some common techniques used in mindfulness and meditation practices include breathing exercises, body scans, visualizations, and guided meditations.

How often should someone practice mindfulness and meditation to see benefits?
While the frequency and duration of mindfulness and meditation practice may vary depending on individual preferences and schedules, it is generally recommended to practice at least once a day for 10-20 minutes to see benefits.

What is the difference between mindfulness and meditation?
Mindfulness is a type of meditation that involves paying attention to the present moment with an open, non-judgmental awareness. Meditation, on the other hand, is a broad term that encompasses various practices and techniques, including mindfulness meditation, focused attention meditation, and loving-kindness meditation.

Quiz Pg 96

How can having supportive friends and family members benefit our mental and emotional well-being?

Answer: c. Both a and b (Provide emotional support and offer practical help and guidance)

What is one way to build and maintain strong connections with others?

Answer: d. All of the above (Be vulnerable, listen actively, and show appreciation)

Can virtual communication platforms be effective in maintaining strong relationships?

Answer: a. Yes

Quiz 117

Why is finding purpose and meaning important after a traumatic event?

d. All of the above - It can help us make sense of what has happened to us, provide us with a sense of control over our lives, and help us build resilience.

Who is an example of someone who found purpose and meaning after trauma?

c. Both a and b - Malala Yousafzai and Elizabeth Smart are both examples of individuals who found purpose and meaning after experiencing trauma.

What is one journal exercise for exploring your sense of purpose and meaning?

d. Write a letter to your future self - Writing a letter to your future self can help you think about your hopes, dreams, and goals and how they relate to your sense of purpose and meaning.

What is resilience?

a. The ability to bounce back from setbacks - Resilience refers to the ability to adapt and bounce back from difficult or challenging situations.

How can purpose and meaning help build resilience?

d. Both a and b - By providing motivation to keep moving forward and a sense of control over our lives, purpose and meaning can help individuals build resilience.

What is a potential benefit of finding purpose and meaning after trauma?

d. All of the above - Finding purpose and meaning after trauma can lead to improved mental health and well-being, increased job satisfaction, and improved relationships with others.

Quiz Page 123

True or False: Finding purpose and meaning after trauma is not important for mental health and well-being.

False

True or False: Having a sense of purpose can lead to increased job satisfaction.

True

What is one potential benefit of finding purpose and meaning after trauma?

Improved mental health and well-being

What is one way to explore your values?

Reflect on experiences and situations that have been important to you, and consider what values they align with

What is one way to explore your passions?

Try new activities or hobbies that you are interested in, and pay attention to what you enjoy and feel fulfilled by

Why might it be helpful to break down larger goals into smaller, more manageable steps?

Breaking down larger goals can make them feel less overwhelming and more achievable, which can increase motivation and reduce stress

True or False: You can only find purpose and meaning in work-related activities.

False

True or False: Finding purpose and meaning after trauma is a one-time event.
False

What is one potential outcome of journaling?

Improved self-awareness and reflection

True or False: Everyone has the same values and passions.

False

Quiz 130

Why is celebrating progress and recognizing accomplishments important?
Answer: d. All of the above

What is one tip for celebrating progress and recognizing accomplishments?
Answer: b. Reflect on the journey and the process

What is the difference between celebrating progress and recognizing accomplishments?
Answer: a. Celebrating progress focuses on the journey, while recognizing accomplishments focuses on the destination.

What are some examples of ways to celebrate progress and recognize accomplishments?
Answer: d. All of the above

What is one benefit of celebrating progress and recognizing accomplishments regularly?
Answer: d. All of the above

True or False: Celebrating progress and recognizing accomplishments is only important for big accomplishments, such as graduating college or getting a promotion.
Answer: b. False

Quiz 161

True or false: The gut and the brain communicate with each other through the vagus nerve.

True

Which of the following foods is a good source of probiotics?
a. White bread
b. Yogurt
c. French fries
d. Potato chips

b. Yogurt

True or false: The Mediterranean diet has been shown to improve mental health outcomes.

True

What is a common gut issue that can affect mental health?
a. Arthritis
b. Psoriasis
c. Irritable bowel syndrome (IBS)
d. Migraines

c. Irritable bowel syndrome (IBS)

Quiz page 171

What is insomnia?
Answer: b. A sleep disorder characterized by difficulty falling or staying asleep.

What is sleep apnea?
Answer: c. A sleep disorder characterized by pauses in breathing or shallow breathing during sleep.

What is restless leg syndrome?
Answer: c. A sleep disorder characterized by uncomfortable sensations in the legs, particularly at night, that often result in an irresistible urge to move them.

What is narcolepsy?
Answer: c. A sleep disorder characterized by sudden and uncontrollable sleep attacks.

Which of the following is NOT a common treatment for sleep disorders?
Answer: c. Surgery

How is sleep apnea diagnosed?
Answer: a. A sleep study that measures brain waves, eye movements, and heart rate during sleep.

What are some common risk factors for sleep apnea?
Answer: d. All of the above. (Being overweight or obese, being a smoker, having a family history of sleep apnea)

What is the recommended amount of sleep for adults?
Answer: c. 8-9 hours per night.

What are some potential consequences of untreated sleep disorders?
Answer: d. All of the above. (High blood pressure, diabetes, depression)

What can you do to improve your sleep hygiene?
Answer: e. All of the above. (Stick to a regular sleep schedule, create a relaxing bedtime routine, avoid caffeine, alcohol, and heavy meals before bedtime, keep your bedroom quiet, dark, and cool)